The
Literary
Almanac

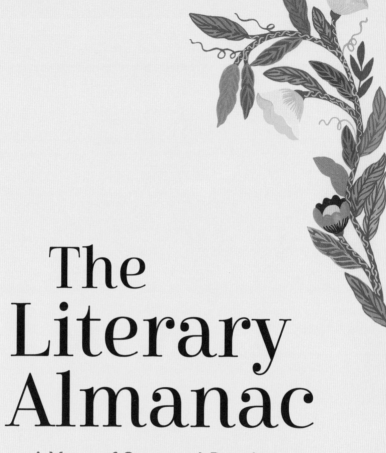

The
Literary
Almanac

A Year of Seasonal Reading

Francesca Beauman

greenfinch

First published in Great Britain in 2021 by
Greenfinch
An imprint of Quercus Editions Ltd
Carmelite House
50 Victoria Embankment
London EC4Y 0DZ

An Hachette UK company

A CIP catalogue record for this book is available from the British Library

HB ISBN 978-1-52941-291-8
eBook ISBN 978-1-52941-292-5

10 9 8 7 6 5 4 3 2 1

Publisher: Kerry Enzor
Project Editor: Melissa Hookway
Design: Tokiko Morishima
Production: Amy Knight

Printed and bound in China by C&C Offset Printing Co. Ltd

MIX
Paper from
responsible sources
FSC® C104740

Papers used by Greenfinch are from well-managed
forests and other responsible sources.

Contents

Introduction

As a child, I used to get into trouble with my parents if I forgot to bring a book with me any time we left the house. The dentist, a long car journey, in a restaurant on holiday: they were doing what they could to shield me from the horrifying prospect of having three minutes to spare with nothing to read. Sometimes, when our family had had a particularly busy or difficult day, my mum and dad would go as far as to compel us to read while we were eating, too: 'Supper's ready, bring your book!', they would shout up the stairs. To others, it may have seemed strange, even unfriendly; I, however, felt like the luckiest girl in the world. Decades later, I maintain a close-to-psychotic compulsion to carry a book around wherever I go. I even took *The Pursuit of Love* by Nancy Mitford with me to the hospital when I went into labour with my first baby – you know, just in case I got bored in between contractions (it won't surprise you to know that I didn't even crack the spine).

Sometimes, though, I wake up in the night worrying about all the books that I won't have time to read before I die. Will I take my last breath wishing I'd spent that long weekend in February immersed in Zadie Smith, rather than irritated by Jonathan Franzen? Entertained by Elizabeth Gaskell rather than filled with ennui by Herman Melville? I mean, probably, yes, but there's nothing I can do about it now. The dilemma of What to Read Next can become overwhelming, can't it? Paralyzing, even. Flummoxed and exhausted by book recommendations from friends, newspapers and social media, you give in and buy the latest new release that 'everyone' says is a masterpiece. However, a couple of chapters in, you find yourself flinging it across the room in frustration, thinking there is something wrong with you. Well, I am here to tell you that it's not you; it's the book. Maybe it's (whisper it) not actually very good; maybe it doesn't suit your current mood, or your current age, or your current pyjamas. And you know what? That's just fine.

'To everything there is a season,' according to chapter three of Ecclesiastes, and books are no exception. Centuries of tradition have made us feel one way in early spring, when the sun peeps out for the first time in ages and the earliest flowers begin to emerge out of the ground, but another way in the dreary days of winter when everyone is hunkered down, eating crisps and feeling depressed. Our reading habits naturally shift accordingly, inspiring us to reach for different kinds of novels at different times of the year.

This is where *The Literary Almanac* comes in. The ultimate reading list for book lovers everywhere, it offers a seasonal structure to take you through the calendar year. Each book has been selected to chime with a specific month, opening our imaginations to the different seasons and rhythms of our world and signposting the passage of time. From *The Count of Monte Cristo* to snuggle up with on long winter nights to *My Brilliant Friend* on the beach in high summer to *Diary of a Provincial Lady* to get you through a family Christmas while eating too much chocolate and trying to avoid chit-chat, I hope you will find oodles of inspiration within these pages. And so, when next faced with the groaning tables of your local bookshop as the shop assistant tries to recommend a new Czech novel in translation ('Although I also have the untranslated version, if you're interested...'), you can instead allow the seasons to guide your choice, rather than your fear of offending the delightful young person in question.

Contained within the pages of *The Literary Almanac* are more than three hundred suggestions of what to read and when. Every book featured is one that I love and adore with a passion and I am confident that you will, too. In my view, the point of reading novels is – well, firstly for fun, but secondly to explain how the world works, to help us understand why people behave the way they do. I can't guarantee that you will want to clutch all of my recommendations to your bosom in joy and admiration, but you will find, I promise, that they open you up to a world of insight and empathy. As you turn to page one of *Childhood* by Tove Ditlevsen in February or *The Moonstone* by Wilkie Collins in October, you can be confident that there is no better time to embark upon that particular reading adventure.

Quite recently, the same daughter to whom I'd given birth while not reading *The Pursuit of Love* insisted on taking one of the longest in Rick Riordan's series of Percy Jackson books to a Beyoncé concert. You know, 'just in case'. I was about to object; I mean, who takes a book to a Beyoncé concert?! But then I realized that we do – our family – that's who. Off we went, my daughter carrying an enormous, heavy hardback under her arm, a picture of a dragon on the cover. To others, it may have seemed strange, even unfriendly; I hope she, however, felt like the luckiest girl in the world.

Francesca Beauman
Bath, Somerset
2021

January
February
March
April
May
June
July
August
September
October
November
December

NEW YEAR'S RESOLUTIONS

First, to have none. Not to be tied.

Second, to be free & kindly with myself, not goading it to parties: to sit rather privately reading in the studio.

To make a good job of The Waves *[the novel Virginia Woolf was writing at the time].*

To care nothing for making money.

As for Nelly [Virginia Woolf's housekeeper], to stop irritation by the assurance that nothing is worth irritation: if it comes back, she must go. Then not to slip this time into the easiness of letting her stay.

Then – well the chief resolution is the most important – not to make resolutions. Sometimes to read, sometimes not to read. To go out yes – but stay at home in spite of being asked. As for clothes, I think to buy good ones.

The Diary of Virginia Woolf
January 2, 1931

There's something very special about being the first. The first woman, the first step, the first bite, the first kiss, the first month. In my experience, January is also the most reading-y (yes, that is the technical term) of months. What else is there to do, post-Christmas? The cupboards are empty, the wine rack is depleted, the bank account is unhappy, and you are a saint if you're able to be in the same room as your significant other without wanting to start a fight (did you know that more people sign up to dating apps on the first Sunday in January than on any other day of the year?). Meanwhile, the nights are long, dark and cold; this is Mother Nature giving you permission to stay snuggled up on the sofa for as long as you like. I suggest you listen to Her.

So, take a deep breath and crack the spine of one of those long, long books you've been meaning to read for years: one full of fun and adventure, with a huge cast of characters and as many locations as a Grand Tour, to which adjectives like 'jolly' and 'rollicking' can be applied. This is not the moment for profundity, obtuseness or abstraction; this is the moment for radiating light like a glimpse of the moon through freshly snow-covered trees.

The aim is for a truly immersive experience: by the time you next raise your head from the page, you will have forgotten that the boiler has broken, there's no hot water, and you can't feel your toes.

The Count of Monte Cristo

BY ALEXANDRE DUMAS (1844, FIRST ENGLISH
TRANSLATION 1846 BY EMMA HARDY)

There seems to be an unspoken law that everyone who sees you reading *The Count of Monte Cristo* has to comment on its length. Having embarked on the more than twelve hundred pages of glorious adventure, you will find yourself not wanting this usually-so-depressing of months to end; your heart will sink when a friend messages you to suggest an outing with actual, real-life people. The horror! There is a whole world of literary excitement that needs you more.

Alexandre Dumas was born in 1802; his mother was the daughter of an innkeeper and his father was the first person of colour to reach the rank of general in the French army. His father inspired many of the themes in Dumas's writing: having been taken prisoner in 1799 during the French Revolutionary Wars, Napoleon left him to languish in captivity until his wife eventually secured his release. He never fully recovered his health, however, and died when Alexandre was just four years old. No military pension was offered; instead, his young son was left with just the memory of a heroic but hugely wronged father. *The Count of Monte Cristo* can thus in some ways be viewed as a revenge fantasy come to life.

The Count of Monte Cristo is an adventure story for which the word 'swashbuckling' was surely invented. It is about a 19-year-old merchant sailor named Edmond Dantes who is wrongly accused of treason and imprisoned on an island in the middle of the sea. Fourteen years later he escapes, uncovers a fortune in buried treasure after a tip-off from the prisoner in the next cell, reinvents himself as the Count of Monte Cristo, then spends years exacting his revenge on those who plotted against him.

And what a thrilling ride it is! Dumas immerses the reader in the most glorious way: be a member of the carnival crowd in Rome, go to the opera in Paris, end up on a treasure island in the middle of the Mediterranean, smoke 'the finest hashish of Alexandria'. The cast of characters includes a female serial poisoner, a drug addict, a secret lesbian, and any number of illegitimate children. The count himself maintains multiple identities and aliases, including Sinbad the Sailor, an English aristocrat named Lord Wilmore, an Italian priest, a banker and a Maltese sailor. As you may imagine, the plot of *The Count of Monte Cristo* is bonkersly complicated, but all the more gripping for the wonderful sense of escapism it offers. Dumas has a terrific line in aphorisms too, for example: 'All human wisdom is contained in these two words – "wait" and "hope".'

This is the sort of book you can only really get into on holiday or in hospital or in jail – that is, when you have a huge amount of time on your hands. Your usual reading routine of ten minutes in bed every night just will not work with a book as long as this, you would never be able to remember who any of the characters are. But that's the thing with long books: the moment when you turn the last page is so rewarding! What a sense of satisfaction, as well as sweet, sweet loss – like you'll miss all the characters as though they were friends.

White Teeth

BY ZADIE SMITH (2000)

N ew Year's Day is the setting for the opening scene of Zadie
Smith's *White Teeth*:

*Early in the morning, late in the century, Cricklewood
Broadway. At 06.27 hours on 1 January 1975, Alfred Archibald
Jones was dressed in corduroy and sat in a fume-filled Cavalier
Musketeer Estate face down on the steering wheel, hoping the
judgement would not be too heavy upon him.*

Yet it turns out that 'it was second-chance time for Archie…'; the
rest of this comic masterpiece by Zadie Smith follows Archie Jones
and his best friend Samad Iqbal – a Bengali Muslim originally from
Bangladesh whom he met when they both served in the same tank
crew during the Second World War – as they and their families
navigate London life in the dying years of the 20th century. *White
Teeth* is, at its heart, a traditional family saga – like a cross between
Salman Rushdie and Elizabeth Jane Howard, but funnier.

Zadie Smith was born in Willesden in north-west London to a
Jamaican mother and an English father. At this point, I need to admit
I have had an intense girl crush on Smith ever since I briefly dated a
friend of hers at university. She was always the cleverest person in
the room and it came as no surprise when she sold *White Teeth* to
a publisher while we were still studying for exams; you bet it was the

talk of the student bar. Okay, please now enjoy the spectacle of me trying, but inevitably failing, not to gush.

Smith is clear with the reader about the theme of the book: 'the myth, the wicked lie, that the past is always tense and the future, perfect. And as Archie knows, it's not like that. It's never been like that.' This is typical of her writing: a play on words that also works on a genuinely profound level. She is able to carve wit and meaning out of a million different combinations of 26 letters to both move and amuse the reader, often within the same sentence. Take this great line, for example: 'Greetings cards routinely tell us everybody deserves love. No. Everybody deserves clean water. Not everybody deserves love all the time.' There is a cynicism wrapped up in a warmth about Smith's world view that I admire and adore.

The north-west London milieu in which the novel is set is very much of its time, just as, say, Anthony Trollope was very much of his time in *The Way We Live Now*. Smith is clearly fascinated by the experience of the children of first-generation immigrants who grow up immersed in tales of their parents' former lives, yet without feeling any real connection to them. Hers is a mostly positive depiction of multiculturalism and how it can work and even triumph within a local community.

White Teeth is a work of huge energy, humour and pace that is sometimes so over-the-top in the best possible way that it genuinely makes you feel happy to be alive. You know the words that best sum it up, though? Joyful. Hopeful. Like a new day is dawning.

Top five books set at New Year

1/*Sir Gawain and the Green Knight*
by an unknown author (14th century)
Travel back to Camelot on New Year's Day, when the feasting knights are interrupted by a green giant up for a fight. Sir Gawain rudely decapitates him, but the giant manages to pick up his own head and challenge Sir Gawain to a return fight in exactly a year. Note: this is a text to flick through for the feel of it, rather than one to read word for word.

2/*Middlemarch*
by George Eliot (1871)
The Vincys throw a 'thoroughly friendly' New Year's Day party: '...the Vincy children all dined at the table... the party was a merry one...the drawing-room was given up to music and games, while whist-tables were prepared in the quiet room on the other side of the hall.' Meanwhile, in the parlour, the children are entranced by a re-telling of the story of Rumpelstiltskin. It is a vivid picture of 19th-century provincial life in this most beloved of books.

3/*The Children of Men*
by P D James (1992)
Warning: not for the easily dispirited. On New Year's Day 2021, the last human to be born on Earth is killed in a pub fight; panic ensues due to a pandemic having made everyone infertile. Desperately dystopian, brilliantly gripping.

4/*Forever*
by Judy Blume (1975)
Soon-to-be young lovers Katherine and Michael meet at a New Year's Eve party, then spend excruciating months trying to decide whether to sleep together. A touching classic of the teenage years, ideally read while hiding from your parents.

5/*Bridget Jones's Diary*
by Helen Fielding (1996)
Like the best kind of lover: funny, surprising and rewards repeated return visits.

Two stories of
snow and solitude

The Alberta Trilogy by Cora Sandel (1926)

A central theme of Cora Sandel's novels, first published in Norway in the 1920s but not translated into English until the 1960s, is the impact of a cold climate on the human heart. The first in the trilogy is called *Alberta and Jacob*: it tells the story of a young woman suffering under the influence of the patriarchy that dominated 19th-century Norwegian society. A houseguest named Frederick asks Alberta, 'You're not going to tell me you can live solely on the light and the memory of a few sun-filled nights and – let us say – tea and a little local gossip and a little handiwork?' And yet millions of young women worldwide nourished their minds and their souls with not much more. Frederick continues, 'But what have you got besides the most banal social life?' What indeed, Alberta wonders, but she is angry and snaps back at him provocatively, 'We have cards and toddy', though afterwards she finds herself feeling grateful towards him for even noticing that she is unhappy. With echoes of many other novels about a bored, stifled young woman trying to escape her circumstances despite what society decrees (*Anna Karenina*, *Madame Bovary*, *My Brilliant Friend*...), but with lots more snow, *The Alberta Trilogy* is a fascinating entry into the canon of Scandinavian literature.

The Secret Scripture by Sebastian Barry (2008)

If your mood for January is less about fluttering snowflakes and more about bitter Irish coffee, then this is the novel for you. Dismal and bleak, just like the month in question can be when viewed from a particular angle, this is the story of an old lady who has been a long-term resident in a mental hospital in the west of Ireland. In interviews, Barry has said that he came up with the idea on a road trip: 'We were driving through Sligo, and my mother pointed out a hut and told me that was where my great-uncle's first wife had lived before being put into a lunatic asylum by the family. She knew nothing more, except that she was beautiful.' This desperately sad and moving novel is the perfect vehicle for Barry's allusive, emotive prose, which is more like poetry really but without the trickiness.

January

February

March
April
May
June
July
August
September
October
November
December

February is a suitable month for dying. Everything around is dead, the trees black and frozen so that the appearance of green shoots two months hence seems preposterous, the ground hard and cold, the snow dirty, the winter hateful, hanging on too long.

Anna Quindlen, *One True Thing* (1994)

U gh, February. What a horrible month it is. Way past Christmas but not yet spring, it is surely only ski enthusiasts who can muster any fondness for it (in the northern hemisphere at least, February does indeed often boast the best snow). For the rest of us, it is a grim and gruelling 28-day slog, definitely justifying its Latin derivation from the word *februare*, meaning to purify or purge. At least it has the decency to be the shortest month of the year. Halfway through, it attempts to atone for its sins by offering up Valentine's Day, but I, for one, won't be tricked by this distraction. I prefer instead to embrace the gloominess. In February I want to read titles that are puritanical in every sense of the word (which is perhaps why I so often reach for Victorian novels in particular) in the knowledge that, with the inexorable passing of the hours and days, change is coming. The occasional sighting of a snowdrop is proof of this, hence they are known in some local areas as 'fair maids of February'.

All we can do is put one foot in front of the other, turn one page after the other, and just get through. On we plod until we spy a glimmer of light, or perhaps even the first bluebells.

The Scarlet Letter

BY NATHANIEL HAWTHORNE (1850)

N athaniel Hawthorne invented a new genre of American literature with *The Scarlet Letter*: the psychological novel. It is bleak. It is melodramatic. It is to be read on a dull, grey afternoon after you've had soup for lunch but before you'll allow yourself a cup of tea and a biscuit.

The novel is set in Massachusetts Bay Colony in the 1640s. We meet Hester Prynne who, after her husband goes to Amsterdam and she doesn't hear from him for two years, falls into a relationship with the pastor that results in a child, Pearl. Hester is punished for her behaviour by the local magistrates, who are considered lenient when they do not sentence her to death. Instead, as a neighbour observes, 'in their great mercy and tenderness of heart, they have doomed Mistress Prynne to stand only a space of three hours on the platform of the pillory, and then and thereafter, for the remainder of her natural life, to wear a mark of shame…' Hester appears on the scaffold having sewn her 'mark of shame' herself: a scarlet-coloured letter A, 'so fantastically embroidered and illuminated upon her bosom. It had the effect of a spell, taking her out of the ordinary relations with humanity, and enclosing her in a sphere by herself.' The rest of her life is spent attempting to redeem herself and her daughter in the eyes of the appallingly judgmental society in which she finds herself trapped.

The style of writing in *The Scarlet Letter* is undoubtedly old-fashioned, but stick with it because it is a fascinating historical document of what life was like in 17th-century New England: how

people spoke, what they wore, the jobs they did, even the plants they used to make medicine. What is most shocking, however, is the code of conduct under which they were all expected to behave. There was certainly no sense of 'live and let live'. The moral rigidity! The hypocrisy! The interfering! And yet, the way society shames those who do not live within its narrow strictures is highly relevant to today – just glance at any number of social media outlets for even a millisecond. One of the book's main themes is the struggle between the law of nature versus the law of man, arguing that the latter is primarily just a social construct to keep everyone in line. Most of all, though, it is a furious attack on Puritanism – both the upper-case kind and the lower-case kind.

When Nathaniel Hawthorne started writing, he certainly had plenty of family history on which to draw for ideas. Born in Salem, Massachusetts, in 1804, his father was a sea captain who died of yellow fever in Dutch Guiana when Nathaniel was four years old. Growing up, he was told all sorts of lurid tales of his father's Puritan ancestors: his great-great-great-grandfather persecuted Quakers and his great-great-grandfather persecuted witches, while one of his mother's ancestors was accused of incest and forced to display herself at the local church with the word 'incest' pinned to her hat.

Hawthorne spent his adult life in the city of Boston, working as a measurer of salt and coal at the Custom House and later as Surveyor of the District of Salem. He was fired from the latter for his political, anti-Puritan views, and it was in the years immediately after this humiliation, while living in poverty and trying to support his wife (the splendidly named Sophie Peabody) and their two children, that he wrote *The Scarlet Letter*. It was an instant hit.

The Scarlet Letter appeared just a couple of years after the first ever women's rights convention in Seneca Falls in New York, and it is perhaps no coincidence that Hester was one of the first heroines to appear in American fiction (if not the first), struggling with herself and her sexuality in a society that seemed to delight in the oppression of women. Under Hawthorne's penmanship, Hester's thoughts have an appealingly timeless quality to them, for example capturing the pain of a relationship break-up: 'How deeply had they known each other then! And was this the man? She hardly knew him now.' We've all been there, darling. You will cheer Hester on as she becomes brilliant at needlework, raises her outspoken daughter alone, and takes the decision not to move away, seeking instead to save herself through good behavior and hard work (not that she should have to, but anyway). Hawthorne takes the radical step of placing a woman's story at the heart of the matter, and what a relief it is.

27

Top ten love stories for
Valentine's Day *(if you really must)*

1/*Dr Zhivago*
by Boris Pasternak (1957)
Oh, how I adore this Russian novel set in the early years of the 20th century about Yury, a medical officer in the army, who falls hopelessly in love with Lara while also dealing with a civil war, too much snow, and endless fur hats.

2/*Me Before You*
by JoJo Moyes (2012)
A warm, sweet, romantic novel: Louisa is hired to care for Will who is paralysed and in a wheelchair, and you will be having a totally cathartic sob before you can even find a box of tissues.

3/*The Well of Loneliness*
by Radclyffe Hall (1928)
This is the story of a little girl who is named Stephen because her parents had wanted a boy, who grows up to realize that she is attracted to women in an era when being a lesbian was thought almost as bad as being a Communist. Set variously in the stately homes of the English upper classes, the battlefields of the First World War, and the streets of bohemian Paris, it is a desperately sad but deeply engrossing account of the hideous challenges Stephen faces as she tries to live her life. I do have one caveat, and it is quite a major one: the writing is sort of terrible. Sentences are clunky and overblown, the sentiments grandiose and melodramatic – but none of this matters. The book is charming, an extraordinary historical document, and genuinely transports you to another time and place.

4/*Strange Weather in Tokyo*
by Hiromi Kawakami (2001)
Thirty-something Tsukiko bumps into one of her old high-school teachers in a bar in Tokyo and soon finds herself in the midst of a delicate, dreamy romance.

5/*The Confessions of Frannie Langton* by Sara Collins (2019)
Born on a slave plantation in Jamaica, lady's maid Frannie Langton embarks on a passionate romance with her French mistress in 19th-century London in this bold, brave, un-boring love story.

6/*Call Me by Your Name*
by André Aciman (2007)
This Italian novel captures the wonder of first love as 17-year-old Elio falls in love with an older friend named Oliver while on holiday. It includes one of my favourite passages about the awful pain of falling in love: 'If there is a pain, nurse it, and if there is a flame, don't snuff it out, don't be brutal with it. Withdrawal can be a terrible thing when it keeps us awake at night... But to feel nothing so as not to feel anything – what a waste.'

7/*Mr Loverman*
by Bernardine Evaristo (2003)
In this lively, subversive evocation of the Caribbean community in East London around the turn of the last century, Evaristo explores a love affair between a 74-year-old Antiguan gentleman and his best male friend from back home.

8/*The Pursuit of Love*
by Nancy Mitford (1945)
Mitford offers up the best piece of advice ever given about the secret to a happy marriage: 'very very great niceness – *gentillesse* – and wonderful good manners.' The book also contains the most romantic scene in literature, in which Linda meets Fabrice on the platform of the Gare du Nord in Paris. Funny and sweet and mildly ridiculous, just like the book itself.

9/*Circling The Sun*
by Paula McLain (2015)
This delicious romance set in Kenya in the 1920s brings to life the story of aviator Beryl Markham as she navigates a complex love triangle between herself, safari hunter Denys Finch Hatton and author of *Out of Africa*, Karen Blixen. Save it for the rainiest of rainy days.

10/*The Transit of Venus*
by Shirley Hazzard (1980)
A beautiful, complex piece of prose about love. Two Australian sisters, Grace and Caro, emigrate to England in the 1950s and embark on a series of relationships with variously suitable and unsuitable men. Even better the second time you read it than the first, if that's possible.

Childhood

BY TOVE DITLEVSEN (1967, FIRST ENGLISH TRANSLATION 1985 BY TIINA NUNNALLY)

D on't you adore a short book? Aren't they just the best? *Childhood* by Tove Ditlevsen, beautifully translated from the Danish by Tiina Nunnally, will open your eyes to another world, expand your knowledge of the human existence, and all in the space of just 99 pages. It's a curriculum classic in Denmark, taught in schools and guaranteed to cause most Danes to light up in delight when you mention it. In the genre of autofiction before autofiction was even a thing, it compares in some ways to better known works like Elena Ferrante's Neapolitan quartet, but with a distinctly Scandinavian tone entirely of its own.

Tove Ditlevsen was born in 1917 in a working-class neighbourhood. As described in *Childhood*, bedrooms were cold, food was scarce, the men were mostly drunk, and women did not write for fun or for money. However, at the age of five Ditlevsen was presented with a book of Grimm's fairytales for Christmas and it opened up a whole new world for her; at the same time, however, her newfound interest in the written word soon made her feel like the odd one out in her community.

Ditlevsen details with wonderful clarity and wit what it was like growing up in a crowded tenement building in 1920s Copenhagen, wrestling along the way with the dual challenges of being both working-class and female. Her prose is deceptively simple, but has a devastating edge to it:

Childhood is dark and it's always moaning like a little animal that's locked in a cellar and forgotten. It comes out of your throat like your breath in the cold, and sometimes it's too little, other times too big. It never fits exactly. It's only when it has been cast off that you can look at it calmly and talk about it like an illness you've survived.

Like all the other girls on her street, Ditlevsen was expected to 'marry a stable skilled worker who doesn't drink, or get a steady job with a pension.' That is not what happened. Here's why: 'Even though no one else cares for my poems, I have to write them because it dulls the sorrow and longing in my heart.' This is typical of the startling directness of the writing in *Childhood*: candid, elegant and powerful. Ditlevsen crafts her sentences with a lack of fussiness that I admire enormously. Descriptive writing often bores me and I tend willfully to skip lengthy paragraphs about the light in the sky or the colour of the water. Yet somehow Ditlevsen is able to circumvent this with vivid image after vivid image.

Ditlevsen's urge to make sense of a sometimes brutal world is a powerful one. She is very precise in the way she captures, without self-pity, the trials and tribulations of being born at a particular time in a particular place. It is as a wordsmith that she feels the most comfortable, placing her in a long tradition of women seeking to express themselves in a society that does not value their sex's right to do so.

Childhood ends with what Ditlevsen perceives to be the end of her childhood, when she is confirmed into the Catholic Church aged 14 and leaves school to go out to work. The rest of her life was tragically overshadowed by depression and drug addiction, but her legacy lives on in *Childhood*, which was the first in a trilogy, followed by *Youth* (also 1967) and *Dependency* (1971). All three stand up against the great works of autobiographical fiction from Sylvia Plath's *The Bell Jar* to Jeanette Winterson's *Oranges Are Not the Only Fruit*, but without the advantage of the Anglo-American literary world to propel them into the limelight.

FEBRUARY BLUES

William Shakespeare conjured up the bleakness often associated with February in *Much Ado About Nothing* when Don Pedro greets Benedick enquiring *'Why, what's the matter,/ That you have such a February face,/ So full of frost, of storm and cloudiness?'*

(Act V, Scene 4)

Two books about coal mining, perhaps the ultimate expression of the journey from the dark into the light

Germinal by Émile Zola (1885)

A friend recommended this to me recently when I was going to France. 'You'll love it,' she told me. 'It's about coal miners in the 19th century.' I apparently looked doubtful. 'Honestly, it's gripping – you'll lose yourself in it completely. All of humanity is there.' She was right. Set in a coal-mining town in northern France in the 1860s, *Germinal* is first of all a fascinating social document about what everyday life was like then: one of my favourite scenes is the songbird competition in the local tavern. More profoundly, it also offers acute insights into male-female relations, employer-employee relations, how a revolution does or does not happen, and plenty more besides. The plot makes this the very definition of a page-turner. I honestly wish it had been three times the length: I could have spent so much more time with Etienne, the hero of the story, and his ragtag bunch of rebels as together they embark on a coal miners' strike to demand better conditions and pay. It is certainly a reminder always to read as widely as possible and refrain from being overly judgmental in one's literary tastes. Because who knew that an entire chapter about the way the pulley system in a coal mine works would be totally, completely, one hundred per cent my jam?

Also
Try

North and South by Elizabeth Gaskell (1854)

This grim, gruelling novel centres upon 19-year-old Margaret Hale, who moves to Manchester and finds herself appalled by the labour conditions of those working in the mines. It offers a radical appraisal of contemporary class and gender identities, as well as a rollicking good plot that includes a compelling romance with Mr Thornton, a local mill owner with whom she butts heads, but – well, you can probably guess what happens. The original title was *Margaret Hale* but Charles Dickens, in whose journal it was first published in serial form, made Gaskell change it to *North and South*, which he felt better represented the themes. It depends on what you think the themes are though, doesn't it, and what is important and significant? *North and South* is <u>the</u> novel of the Industrial Revolution: acutely aware, quietly cross, and highly insightful about how the personal and the political are always intertwined. Don't worry though, it still ends with a marriage proposal, like all the best 19th-century novels.

A few favourite short story collections *to celebrate the shortest month of the year*

Attrib. and other stories by Eley Williams (2017)

•

Selected Stories by Anton Chekhov (1932)

•

Grand Union by Zadie Smith (2019)

•

The Portable Dorothy Parker by Dorothy Parker (1944)

•

Kiss Kiss by Roald Dahl (1960)

•

Interpreter of Maladies by Jhumpa Lahiri (1999)

•

The Garden Party and Other Stories
by Katherine Mansfield (1922)

•

The Quarry by Ben Halls (2020)

•

Good Evening, Mrs. Craven: the wartime stories of Mollie Panter-Downes by Mollie Panter-Downes (1999)

•

Nudibranch by Irenosen Okojie (2019)

Timeline: A brief whizz through some of the highlights in the history of the development of the American novel *prior to* The Scarlet Letter *in 1850*

1740 The first novel ever to be published in America was an English one: *Pamela* by Samuel Richardson. It is bonkers, but fascinating. Written from the point of view of a 16-year-old maidservant Pamela, it is very much 'Me Too' in its themes, placing an emphasis on the thoughts and feelings of a single individual in a manner that was genuinely innovative for its time.

1789 The first American novel is generally considered to be William Hill Brown's *The Power of Sympathy*, quickly followed by Susanna Rowson's *Charlotte Temple* (1791) and Hannah Webster Foster's *The Coquette* (1797). The plots of all three centre upon a strikingly similar narrative of a woman who allows herself to be seduced, leading to her tragic downfall. Spot a theme here?

1798 *Wieland* by Charles Brockden Brown, a Gothic novel about a brother and sister who begin to hear strange voices.

1824 *Hobomok* by Lydia Maria Child, a historical novel set in New England about a teenage girl who has a relationship with a Native American.

1826 *Last of the Mohicans* by James Fenimore Cooper, an adventure story about two young women on a perilous journey through Native American territory in search of their father.

1830 *Clarence* by Catharine Sedgwick, a novel of manners about a young woman in New York City searching for a husband.

January
February

March

April
May
June
July
August
September
October
November
December

It was one of those March days when the sun
shines hot and the wind blows cold: when it is
summer in the light, and winter in the shade.

Charles Dickens, *Great Expectations* (1861)

I t is a tricky one, March: sort of neither here nor there, you are past the worst of winter but not yet able to revel in the joys of spring. It is a waiting game. Then you wake up one morning and it is about 10 per cent lighter out than it was the day before. Sometimes there is a last tempest of snow, after which you start to see buds pushing through the moss on your morning run and you realize you can wear one less layer on your evening walk.

Named after Mars, the Roman god of war, March used to be the first month of the year; it was only when the Roman calendar was replaced with the Gregorian calendar that it forfeited this honour. The 19th-century American poet Henry Wadsworth Longfellow imagined March's chagrin in his poem, 'The Poet's Calendar':

I Martius am! Once first, and now third!
To lead the Year was my appointed place;
A mortal dispossessed me by a word,
And set there Janus with the double face.

The month also hosts an equinox, which is when the sun is to be found directly over the equator and thus the day and the night are of equal duration. This marks the start of spring in the northern hemisphere and of autumn in the southern hemisphere, and with it a powerful sense of new beginnings.

So, what does this mean for the books on our bedside table? I would like to propose it is a time to turn inwardly, focusing on stories of a philosophical nature or that encourage us to think about the world in a new way. At the same time, while in this sober frame of mind, Mother Nature is telling us to move forward, feel a sense of hope, and emerge out of the darkness. May as well do as She says.

EXPECTATION

March is the Month of Expectation.
The things we do not know –
The Persons of prognostication
Are coming now –
We try to show becoming firmness –
But pompous Joy
Betrays us, as his first Betrothal
Betrays a Boy.

Emily Dickinson,
'March is the Month of Expectation'
(Undated)

The Waiting Years

BY FUMIKO ENCHI (1957, FIRST ENGLISH
TRANSLATION 1971 BY JOHN BESTER)

I am ashamed that I did not read this contemplative, interior novel sooner, but in my defence it was only re-issued in an English edition in 2019. Fumiko Enchi's novel is as insightful about the role of women in society as any number of Anglo-American texts that we may know; it just happens to have been originally written in Japanese.

Fumiko Enchi was a pseudonym used by Fumiko Ueda. Born in Tokyo in 1905, her father was a well-respected philologist at Tokyo University. She was ill as a child and unable to go to school, so she was taught at home, where her grandmother on her mother's side introduced her to classics of Japanese literature.

Early on, Enchi mostly wrote plays; it was only after the collapse of her marriage, a hysterectomy due to uterine cancer, and the destruction of her house in an Allied bombing raid in 1945, that she turned to prose. *The Waiting Years* was her first major novel, written between 1949 and 1957, a howl of rage in response to so much trauma. She went on to publish more than one hundred works and it is surely no coincidence that she found her voice during the Showa era, a period defined by the kind of patriarchal, imperial values against which she sought to rebel in her writing. Sadly, only three of her works have been translated into English, hence her relative lack of international attention. She died in 1986, at the age of 81.

The Waiting Years is set over thirty years from the 1890s onwards. It has an extraordinary premise: the central character, Tomo, is

instructed by her husband to find him a mistress. 'To call the girl a concubine would be making too much of it', he tells her. 'She'll be a maid for you, too...' This was normal for 19th-century, middle-class Japanese women, and the subservience that was expected of them was astonishing. Tomo's feelings were deemed irrelevant; in fact, she wasn't meant to have any feelings. But she does, of course.

A major theme in Enchi's work is the difference between the public self and the private self. Like Cora Sandel in 1920s Norway, Elena Ferrante in contemporary Italy, and many other women writers along the way, she exposes the often shocking gap between what goes on in a woman's head and what she presents to the world. This is a very quiet novel about what occurs behind closed doors.

Near the end, Tomo walks home in the snow after going to visit a former member of the household. She passes small houses, second-hand shops, and general stores, and feels a sudden, futile despair at her compliance in putting her family's honour before everything else, including, and in particular, her own needs:

Was it possible, then, that everything she had lived for was vain and profitless? No: she shook her head in firm rejection of the idea. Her world was a precarious place...yet at the end of it all a brighter world surely lay waiting, like the light when one finally emerges from a tunnel...

Which in many ways of course, also perfectly sums up the month of March. *The Waiting Years* is fascinating sociologically about the Japan of the past, as well as touching and unforgettable about the futility of its heroine's life. But faintly, faintly, like the light brushing of a feather, there are intimations that change is coming. It is, ultimately, a very hopeful book.

Ralph Ellison
Innovator extraordinaire

If March is for exploring books of a philosophical bent in order to help us look inward, let's surely include the writing of Ralph Ellison, who was born on the first of the month. Named after the 19th-century thinker Ralph Waldo Emerson, whom his parents admired, Ralph Waldo Ellison was born in Oklahoma City. His excellent trumpet playing helped him get into university and he soon developed a passionate interest in communism, which is partly explored in *Invisible Man* (1952), the only full-length novel Ellison published.

Invisible Man took Ellison five years to write. T S Eliot's modernist poem 'The Waste Land' was a great source of inspiration, as were the works of Ernest Hemingway. Hence, *Invisible Man* is less the sort of social protest novel that many of his contemporaries were writing, more a piece of experimental literary fiction.

Focus on...

Ellison's narrator is invisible in many senses: literally so because he lives underground beneath the city streets, but also because, he argues, white society views him, as a black man, as a collection of stereotypes rather than an actual person. The central theme, therefore, is the search for identity – which is arguably the central theme of all novels, in fact.

The Three-Body Problem

BY CIXIN LIU (2006, FIRST ENGLISH TRANSLATION 2014 BY KEN LIU)

I f March is a month for thinking about the world in a new way, then *The Three-Body Problem* is the perfect book to have by your side. I will not dissemble: this is a hilariously difficult novel to tackle. It sometimes feels overwhelming, and not just physically (even the paperback is a fairly hefty beast). But do not let that put you off. I started it, then I stopped – it was all a bit much. Then I started it again, then stopped. Then I had a break for a few days, and when I returned to it, oh! what marvels ensued. Very few books offer the mind-bending experience that this one does. It is a stunningly imagined work of science fiction, enormous in both scope and scale.

The three-body problem of the title is a term in physics used to describe modelling the motion of three particles according to Newton's laws. That Cixin Liu uses this as the starting point for a compelling plot about extra-terrestrial life in a distant galaxy is one of the great joys of the novel.

Liu weaves together history (the book starts during the Cultural Revolution of 1967), contemporary politics, and degree-level maths and physics to offer up a gigantic epic that has commonalities with old-school, Western sci-fi writers such as Arthur C Clarke and Isaac Asimov. Yet it is also very much a product of the time and place in which it was written, not least in its emphasis on ecological activism. Unfortunately, its gender politics are suspect (for example, it opens with a distasteful description of the sacrifice of a teenage girl);

characterization is not Liu's strong point, he is more about ideas and events (which, to be clear, is an explanation, not an excuse).

Liu was born in Beijing in 1963. His mother was a primary school teacher and his father was a manager at the Coal Mine Design Institute. He had a life-changing experience aged seven while staying with his grandparents in the countryside: 'Together, we gazed up at the clear night sky, where a tiny star slowly glided across the dark firmament. It was the first artificial satellite China had ever launched: Dong-fanghong I ("The East is Red I"). The date was 25 April 1970.'

From then on, Liu dreamed of being an astronaut, but for all practical purposes this seemed out of reach, so he decided to write instead, inspired in part by a gift from his father of a copy of *Journey to the Centre of the Earth* by Jules Verne (1871). He worked as a computer engineer at a hydroelectric plant in Shanxi in north-west China for many years while writing in his spare time; it was not until 2012, after publishing seven novels including *The Three-Body Problem*, that he gave up his day job.

It is surely no coincidence that science fiction has become hugely popular in China at a time of head-spinningly fast industrial advance; the same happened in Britain in the late 19th century, when the likes of H G Wells's *The War of the Worlds* (1898) seemed to match the national mood in a similar way. This kind of literature is apparently often a response to the feeling that anything could happen.

Persevere with *The Three-Body Problem*. Once you are into it, you are into it. Just do not expect to be able to give an answer to friends who ask, 'What's it about?' Instead, simply lend them your copy of the book and wish them luck. Much like the month of March, it rewards everyone plentifully in the end.

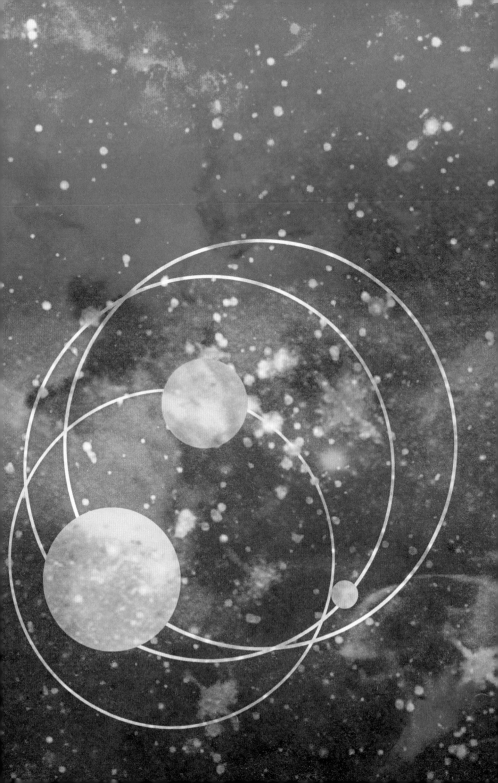

Two more books about the importance of hope

Grief Is the Thing with Feathers by Max Porter (2015)

The title takes its inspiration from the Emily Dickinson poem, '"Hope" Is the Thing with Feathers', and while it is an extremely sad novel, it is also very much about hope, as well as light. Two young boys are struggling with the grief of their mother's death while in the care of their father, a Ted Hughes scholar. The family is frequently visited by a crow, who explains his role in their life thus: 'I was friend, excuse, *deus ex machina*, joke, symptom, figment, spectre, crutch, toy, phantom, gag, analyst and babysitter.' Porter offers the reader space to think about the composition of grief; this is a sparse, airy book, closer to poetry than prose in many ways. It is particularly brilliant about the sense of absence. Language is Porter's plaything and he approaches it like a little boy who has been given a Lego train set for Christmas: joyfully, intensely, uncompromisingly.

The Maias by Eça de Queiróz (1888)

Imagine Charles Dickens, but in Portuguese. A classic 19th-century tale about falling in love with a sister you did not know you had. Happens to the best of us, right? Set mostly in Lisbon in the 1870s, the story centres upon young aristocrat Carlos da Maia and his best friend João da Ega. Many of the greatest novels are, when it comes down to it, really about friendship as the greatest form of love, and this is no exception. Another theme is the extent to which life in Portugal is old-fashioned and backward compared to that of the rest of Europe. 'Here we import everything,' da Ega declares. 'Ideas, laws, philosophies, theories, plots, aesthetics, sciences, style, industries, fashions, manners, jokes, everything arrives in crates by steamship.' *The Maias* also has one of my favourite endings, combining naturalism and symbolism in the most appealing of ways. Hope prevails.

Top ten books that, *like* The Waiting Years, offer an alternative perspective on marriage

1/*The Way Things Are*
by E M Delafield (1927)
I re-read this book often, in part because it includes a favourite line of mine: 'A vague recollection of a sentence, read somewhere, to the effect that it is always the wife and mother who is primarily responsible for the atmosphere of the home, depressed Laura's spirits.' Make of that what you will.

2/*Half of a Yellow Sun*
by Chimamanda Ngozi Adichie (2006)
The author questions the very nature of marriage in this spectacular novel set during the civil war in Nigeria in the late 1960s.

3/*American Wife*
by Curtis Sittenfeld (2008)
Imagine your husband becomes president of the United States. How would it affect your relationship with him, but also with yourself? This is a very clever, sophisticated, humane portrait of a marriage lived in the public eye.

4/*The Guest Cat*
by Takashi Hiraide (2014)
This gorgeous Japanese novel is about a thirty-something, somewhat disconnected couple, both writers, who move into a rented guesthouse on a large estate and befriend a cat. It may not sound like much of a plot, yet Hiraide finds pure poetry in the everyday in this plain, spare tale.

5/*The Weather in the Streets*
by Rosamond Lehmann (1936)
A tale that deftly explores the inner life of Olivia Curtis in the aftermath of a failed marriage. What does she want? What do any of us want? Especially when it comes to men. An elegant and beautifully written novel.

6/*The Portrait of a Lady*
by Henry James (1881)
In which Isabel Archer inherits a load of cash and finds herself entangled with a number of suitors. Ostensibly about marriage but really about power and control. A masterpiece of dazzling insight.

7/ Dept. of Speculation

by Jenny Offill (2014)
The characters have no names, the plot has no context, the story is told in fragments, here and there, piece by piece. And yet there is a magic to this slim novel about a couple who have recently had a baby – like the cleverest, pithiest WhatsApp messages you've ever received, but pieced together in a way that will bring you to tears.

8/Greenery Street

by Denis Mackail (1925)
A rare book that celebrates a happy marriage, this is a sweet, low-key tale of one couple's first year together living in a terraced house in London in the 1920s.

9/So Long a Letter

by Mariama Bâ (1981)
A widow writes to her best friend in the aftermath of her husband's fatal heart attack, in particular about the impact that the traditional practice of polygamy had on her and her life. Enormously interesting about women's lives in Senegal in the 1970s and 1980s, this book addresses a myriad of issues around gender, class and colonialism.

10/The Long View

by Elizabeth Jane Howard (1956)
A portrait of a marriage told backwards from the 1950s to the 1920s. Howard is a writer of quiet genius.

January
February
March

April

May
June
July
August
September
October
November
December

April is the cruellest month breeding
Lilacs out of the dead land, mixing
Memory and desire, stirring
Dull roots with spring rain.

T S Eliot, 'The Waste Land' (1922)

C heer up, T S Eliot! While it is true that April is a month of contradictions, it also has much to recommend it. It begins with April Fool's Day, usually features Easter somewhere along the way, and throughout the visibly changing season offers a glimpse of better things to come: it is a time full of energy and optimism.

April is generally thought to have derived its name from the Latin verb *aperire*, meaning 'to open', in recognition that it is at this time of year that the flowers in the garden begin to open up, along with your heart and mind as you breathe a sigh of relief at what has often felt like a long, long winter. Mother Nature is all of a sudden yelling for your attention, refusing to allow you to ignore Her. This is a time of change, rebirth and renewal.

At this point in the calendar year, the weather is a near-constant topic of conversation in the northern hemisphere. It is often comically unpredictable, switching from sunshine to rain in a matter of minutes and catching you without your raincoat so that you get drenched right away, leaving you feeling cleansed, refreshed and lighter in spirit. Let's try to make sure our reading matter matches its promise.

Weather

BY JENNY OFFILL (2020)

This marvellous, terrifying novel is ostensibly about a woman living in New York with her husband and young son; really, though, it is about the impact of the climate crisis on our mental health.

Weather's protagonist, Lizzie, works on the helpdesk in a library; she also has a part-time job answering the hundreds of letters sent to her former graduate supervisor who now hosts a popular podcast about climate change. She is, perhaps, the only fictional character living in present-day Brooklyn in a not-entirely-happy marriage who doesn't make me want to cry with boredom because I have read about the likes of her so many millions of times before. By some miracle, Offill manages to imbue Lizzie with such charm and appeal that the reader is genuinely thrilled to be in her brain as she ponders worries both large and small. She feels a lack of connection with her husband Ben, her son Eli tells her not to walk him into school any more, her brother is addicted to opioids, her job is stressful and her knee hurts when she goes up stairs. Meanwhile, the reader marvels at the astonishingly precise character description: 'My mother calls and speaks to me of the light, the vine, the living bread.'

Weather is one of the first novels to address the issue of the climate crisis directly and from a deeply human perspective, rather than through the alienating lens of, say, a zombie apocalypse. It forces us to face our anxiety, but at the same time it is hilariously realistic about the way it so often ends up on the long list of all the other things the average adult worries about in a day, as captured in Lizzie's chat with a new acquaintance with whom she's flirting in a bar:

> *And then somehow, it's four drinks later, and I'm telling him about the coming chaos. 'What are you afraid of?' he asks me, and the answer, of course, is dentistry, humiliation, scarcity...*

This is typical of the way *Weather* progresses in fragments, shards, moments of intensity that blaze across the page with a laugh of recognition or a pang of pain.

What sets this highly original and entertaining novel apart is its form. Offill has named as influences experimentalists such as the poet John Berryman and the novelist Gilbert Sorrentino, both of whom played hugely with form, as well as style; her genius is to make this technique so accessible and fun to read. Her prose is redolent of poetry, boasting a highly distinctive style of short paragraphs and even shorter sentences. Each is polished to perfection like the chorus in a song and with this Offill manages to be both brilliantly funny and bitingly sad at the same time.

> *I get a series of ecstatic texts from a newly divorced friend who has met someone. 'I can only imagine what it would be like to be this age and then suddenly fall in love,' I tell Ben. 'You are in love,' he corrects me.*

It is the perfect choice of the word 'corrects' that gets me every time.

Weather is literary fiction that is neither pretentious nor 'difficult'. Sure, it is by no means a cheery read – what book about the climate crisis could be? But it is, counter-intuitively, a genuinely life-affirming one.

Howards End

BY E M FORSTER (1910)

One of my favourite facts about E M Forster is that he wrote all six of his novels in the first 45 years of his life; the second 45 years were spent in other sorts of creative endeavour, such as publishing non-fiction and falling in love. He told the poet Siegfried Sassoon this was because 'my patience with ordinary people has given out'. And yet it is precisely in his writing of 'ordinary people' that Forster reveals his genius: a profound understanding of human nature. Rather like reading Shakespeare's *King Lear*, you read *Howards End* and think, 'but nothing has changed!' It is, in essence, a plea for tolerance: each new day is another chance to make the world better and brighter.

Howards End is about two families, the Schlegels and the Wilcoxes. The Schlegels are of German origin: civilized, literary, funny, talkative, left-leaning, artistic and in some respects very like Forster's Bloomsbury Group companions Virginia Woolf and Vanessa Bell when they were young. The Schlegel sisters, Margaret and Helen, become friends with the Wilcoxes on holiday, even though it is soon clear that they could not be more different in terms of their values and priorities. The Schlegels represent liberal humanism, along with all its associated values of nonconformity, artistic expression and one's inner life; the Wilcoxes, on the other hand, represent the diametric opposite and are pure capitalists. When Mrs Wilcox dies she leaves her house, Howards End, to Margaret in her will. You can imagine the complications that ensue.

The marriage of Margaret Schlegel and Henry Wilcox is central to the success of this novel. Why on earth does Margaret, one of literature's most excellent introverts, want to marry such a shallow bore, the reader asks? Forster offers us a clue in this famous passage from the book:

> It was here that Margaret hoped to help him. It did not seem so difficult. She need trouble him with no gift of her own. She would only point out the salvation that was latent in his own soul, and in the soul of every man. Only connect! That was her whole sermon. Only connect the prose and the passion, and both will be exalted, and human love will be seen at its height.

In other words, we are all humans just trying to get along and do our best; what really matters in life is the bringing together of different value sets, asserting values of tolerance, and Margaret herself likes to practise what she preaches, not least in her choice of partner. The struggle to 'only connect' is made all the more challenging by the ongoing assault on life in Edwardian England of industrialization and urbanization – in other words, of 'progress'.

Howards End is a comedy about the absurdities of social convention, specifically about the awfulness of the English. It tells a good story (because Forster is never dull) and it vividly conjures up life in Edwardian London. But it is the quality of the writing that will astonish you: you could quote every sentence and it will make your heart turn over with the beauty of it. It is funny, wise and devastatingly perceptive. Several decades after *Howards End* was first published, Forster offered up his own assessment: 'Very elaborate and all-pervading plot that is seldom tiresome or forced, range of characters, social sense, wit, wisdom, colour.' He was not wrong.

.

Two books about change

The Garden of the Finzi-Continis
by Giorgio Bassani (1962)

In the garden and on the tennis court of the Finzi-Contini family, the narrator of this entrancing Italian novel becomes infatuated with 23-year-old Micol. This study of first love is, however, overshadowed by dark, stormy clouds. It takes place over the course of eight months in 1938 as Mussolini's racial laws abruptly threaten the way of life of members of the prosperous Jewish community in Ferrara, Italy. The novel reads as a desperately sad memorial for a society that would shortly be totally extinguished, along with most of the protagonists. But it is a memorial full of life: the life of those Ferrara Jews with their games of tennis, their bicycling and their literary and political chat. Throughout, the garden functions as a powerful metaphor for what passes away, and yet what will always remain. This is a novel to read slowly and with attention; an often dense work, it yields even more of its ironies the second time around.

Also Try

The Enchanted April
by Elizabeth von Arnim (1922)

One spring, four rather different women answer a classified ad in *The Times*:

> *To Those who Appreciate Wisteria and Sunshine. Small mediaeval Italian Castle on the shores of the Mediterranean to be let Furnished for the month of April. Necessary servants remain.*

It would seem that English women of a certain sort in this period were all in desperate need of a holiday; as Mrs Wilkins explains to Mrs Arbuthnot, 'Why, it would really be being unselfish to go away and be happy for a little, because we could come back so much nicer.' Mrs Arbuthnot, for whom the highlight of an average day was a dispiriting trip to the fishmongers, agrees. Together they end up in Portofino, Italy, and this funny, charming and easy-going novel becomes a powerful advertisement for the transformative power of a holiday.

Top ten novels that, *like* Howards End, are centred upon a house

1/*Montpelier Parade*
by Karl Geary (2017)
A Georgian terraced house in an affluent part of Dublin is the setting for an intense, unconventional love affair between 16-year-old schoolboy Sonny, who works part-time in the butcher's, and a beautiful, wealthy, older woman named Vera: 'The walls were high, the cornices seemed to float, and the pictures on the wall were not pictures of the pictures, even that you knew.' I first became obsessed with this novel because it is a rare example of a piece of fiction written in the second person, a stylistic decision that is initially unsettling but ultimately kind of awesome.

2/*The Tenant of Wildfell Hall*
by Anne Brontë (1848)
Imagine Charlotte and Emily are your sisters; you'd feel obliged to produce at least one novel, wouldn't you? If only to be part of the gang. This underrated story about a mysterious young widow with a young son who arrives at the aforementioned house is particularly interesting for its early feminist approach.

3/*Cloudstreet*
by Tim Winton (1991)
Imagine Charles Dickens wrote an episode of *Neighbours*. Two down-on-their-luck families, the Pickles and the Lambs, are forced to share a delipidated house at No. 1 Cloudstreet in Perth, Australia, in the years following the Second World War.

4/*I Capture the Castle*
by Dodie Smith (1948)
The cosiest, cup-of-tea-in-bed-in-your-pyjamas book ever.

5/*Golden Hill*
by Francis Spufford (2016)
In this tremendously fun historical novel, a young man from London steps off a boat in New York City in 1746, immediately impressed by how great the city smells compared to his home town: 'no deep patination of filth, no cloacal rainbow for the nose in shades of brown, no staining of the air in sewer dyes'. He heads directly to a counting house to exchange a bill for £1,000 – a counting house that turns out to be full of surprises...

6/The Great Gatsby
by F Scott Fitzgerald (1925)
Jay Gatsby's house is central to this Jazz Age tale of envy. It is described by narrator Nick Carraway as 'a colossal affair by any standard – it was a factual imitation of some Hotel de Ville in Normandy, with a tower on one side, spanking new under a thin beard of raw ivy, and a marble swimming pool...' *The Great Gatsby* is not as good as it thinks it is, but still worth reading.

7/The Dutch House
by Ann Patchett (2019)
A gorgeous family saga that reads like a classic already. Set in suburban Philadelphia, two siblings move into the mansion at the heart of this epic story that begins in the 1940s and spans five decades. Patchett includes a rare depiction in literature of a mother who makes the choice to leave her children in the care of their father (she instead moves to India to help the poor).

8/Lady Audley's Secret
by Mary Elizabeth Braddon (1862)
Set at a stately home known as Audley Court, this fabulously over-the-top thriller relates the tale of a young woman who commits bigamy by mistake, pushes her first husband down a well, poisons her second husband, and sets fire to a hotel – and

that's just the headlines. It contains a few favourite quotes of mine too, for example: 'As if happiness were not essentially accidental – a bright and wandering bird, utterly irregular in its migration; with us one summer's day, and for ever gone from us the next!'

9/The Leopard
by Giuseppe Tomasi di Lampedusa (1958)
Essentially a domestic drama about property inheritance, *The Leopard* opens with a detailed description of the drawing room in which the Prince of Salina and his family like to pray: 'even the parrots spreading iridescent wings over the silken walls appeared unabashed...' But as the narrative unfolds, it becomes clear that this is a house in decline, a family in decline, and more than anything a society in decline. Best read by a swimming pool in Sicily while snacking on *panelle*.

10/Dusty Answer
by Rosamond Lehmann (1927)
A teenage girl is entranced by the children who come and stay in the house next door every summer: 'all boys except one, who was a girl, and who dropped over the peach-tree wall into Judith's garden with invitations to tea and hide-and-seek'. This atmospheric classic of lesbian literature is a delight.

January
February
March
April

May

June
July
August
September
October
November
December

*The month of May was come, when every lusty
heart beginneth to blossom, and to bring forth
fruit; for like as herbs and trees bring forth fruit
and flourish in May, in likewise every lusty heart
that is in any manner a lover, springeth and
flourisheth in lusty deeds. For it giveth unto all
lovers courage, that lusty month of May.*

Sir Thomas Malory, *Le Morte d'Arthur* (1485)

I n many countries throughout Europe and North America, the
month of May begins with May Day, an ancient festival celebrating
spring. The month borrows its name from the Greek goddess
Maia, commonly associated with fertility and growth. The longer days,
warmer evenings, and sights so clichéd that you sometimes wonder
whether they are real – lambs actually frolicking in actual fields – are
a constant reminder that spring has fully arrived. Let our reading reflect
this, telling stories full of *joie de vivre*, passion and playfulness.

With its associations of new life, nurturing and fecundity, it is
appropriate that many countries around the world celebrate Mother's
Day in May. (An exception is the United Kingdom where the date is
linked to the Christian celebration of Lent and is normally observed
in March.) In the knowledge that mothering can take many forms, all
of which are crucial to a functioning society, let us celebrate the books
that celebrate the human instinct to love and nurture in the broadest
sense. It is rare, anyway, to come across a novel specifically about
giving birth; one exception is *The Squire* by Enid Bagnold (1938),
about a 44-year-old upper-middle-class woman who is pregnant with
her fifth child during her husband's absence in India. The scene when

she first meets her baby is written from the point of view of the participant rather than the onlooker and was truly radical for its time:

'So it was you!' said the squire to him, thinking of her nine months' companion, of her hardness towards him, now melted, of his quirks and movements to which she had grown so used, and thinking with wonderment, 'So it was you.'

Whether it is *storge*, *agápe*, *éros*, *philía*, *philautia*, *xenia*, *ludus* or *pragm* (to continue the Greek theme), love is the one emotion that everybody on the planet can understand. From parental adoration to passionate love affairs to long-standing friendships, May is the moment to embrace it all. Because in the end, surely that is why we are all here in the first place, isn't it? To love and be loved?

The Home-Maker

BY DOROTHY CANFIELD FISHER (1924)

An instant success on publication, *The Home-Maker* by Dorothy Canfield Fisher is set in small-town New England. It is the story of Eva, who is almost literally dying of boredom as a stay-at-home mother, and her husband Lester, who detests his job in accounts at a department store and wishes he could spend more time with his children. When Lester falls off a roof and breaks his back, the pair are forced to swap roles and what wondrous happiness ensues! It is one of the great books about being a parent, or a child – or, indeed, a human.

Dorothy Canfield Fisher was born in 1879; her parents, who were academics, named her after Dorothea in George Eliot's *Middlemarch*. She lived in Vermont most of her life with her husband and two children, producing a total of 22 novels and 18 non-fiction works. She is also notable for having introduced the Montessori method of child-rearing to the American public through a series of books and speeches, a passion that very much informed her writing and, in particular, the thoughtful approach to adult–child relationships that is celebrated in *The Home-Maker*.

The month that takes its name from the Greek goddess Maia is the perfect moment to settle down with Fisher's warm, insightful novel. One of the central themes is what it means to nurture, whether as a biological mother or father, a caregiver, a friend, a godparent, or all the other forms of adult input that are so valuable to a child's development. Take the incident where five-year-old Stephen explains

to his father how devastated he feels at the prospect of being forced to wash his favourite teddy bear. In response, his father feels 'horrified... at the position in which he found himself, absolute arbiter over another human being, a being who had no recourse, no appeal from his decisions...' It is a plea to remember that children are humans, too, and experience the full gamut of emotions just as adults do. This does not mean that permissiveness is the way forward, but instead the key to all successful, empathetic interactions is this: talk less, listen more. And thus, Dorothy Canfield Fisher positions herself as a quiet revolutionary, albeit one who will also offer you a cup of fresh coffee and a slice of apple pie (home-made, of course).

Fisher's genius is to persuade the reader to sympathize with all of the characters equally – well, apart from the horrid neighbour, Mrs Anderson. It is this willingness to embrace life's complexities that makes the novel so profoundly moving. Boasting a zippy plot, the gender politics examined here are also astonishingly ahead of their time, throwing new light on the very modern dilemma of how couples ought to organize their domestic life.

In another memorable scene, Mrs Anderson demands to know how Lester copes with having to clean the kitchen floor every day, a task that had previously brought Eva close to despair. Lester's solution?

The attic was piled to the eaves with old newspapers. Every day [an older child] Helen or Henry brings down a fresh supply. We spread them around two or three thick, drop our grease on them with all the peace of mind in the world, whisk them up at night before Eva comes in, and have a spotless floor to show her. What's the matter with that?

What's the matter indeed. I think of this marvellously funny, subversive scene often. It's a reminder of the importance of consistently questioning convention: just because things have always been done a certain way does not necessarily mean that it is the best way. Re-read *The Home-Maker* every May for an invigorating new perspective on the domestic sphere.

TO LOVE AND BE LOVED

I have perceiv'd that to be with those I like is enough,
To stop in company with the rest at evening is enough,
To be surrounded by beautiful, curious, breathing,
laughing flesh is enough,
To pass among them or touch any one, or rest my arm
ever so lightly round his or her neck for a moment,
what is this then?
I do not ask any more delight, I swim in it as in a sea.

Walt Whitman,
'I Sing the Body Electric' (1855)

Never Let Me Go

BY KAZUO ISHIGURO (2005)

My name is Kathy H. I'm thirty-one years old, and I've been a carer now for eleven years. That sounds long enough, I know, but actually they want me to go on for another eight months, until the end of the year.

The opening lines of *Never Let Me Go* set the tone right away for this inimitable novel about what it means to be human, as well as what it means to love. Who are 'they'? Why the specificity of 'another eight months'? What kind of 'carer'? Kathy's apparent straightforwardness belies a sinister tale to tell.

As a child, Kathy attended a private boarding school called Hailsham. All the children there had been brought into the world for a very specific, very alarming purpose, which is gently and slowly revealed to maximum effect over the course of the book. Kathy's two best friends, Ruth and Tommy, think they can escape their hideous fate if they can prove they are in love. This is science fiction, but with a love story at its heart: love for others, love for ourselves, love for the human race as we know it.

The language employed is a masterful combination of childlike with creepy. Told entirely in the first person from the point of view of Kathy, who remains highly literal-minded even after she reaches adulthood, the novel is a quick, easy read. These children are leading very strange lives, but the dialogue makes them seem relatively normal

– until, that is, you stop to think about it for even one second, at which point the reader becomes complicit and the everyday activity starts to seem all the more unsettling. It is almost psychotically understated: there is no drama, but then you realize that every single moment in these children's lives is drama.

Never Let Me Go is also a coming-of-age novel, in some senses not unlike classics of the genre, such as Alain-Fournier's *Le Grand Meaulnes* (1913) or Rosamond Lehmann's *Invitation to the Waltz* (1932), in its themes, but with more clones and fewer hats. Considering an incident at school, Kathy comments 'I'm sure somewhere in your childhood, you too had an experience like ours that day; similar if not in the actual details, then inside, in the feelings...' The pupils of Hailsham experience a version of what all children go through on the journey out of innocence, but in a far more extreme fashion.

It is instructive in this context to remember that Kazuo Ishiguro was born in Nagasaki, in Japan, in 1954, but moved to the UK with his family at the age of five when his father, a physical oceanographer, was offered a job there. No wonder one of the central themes of *Never Let Me Go* is the search for identity; just like all of us to some degree, the pupils at Hailsham are trying to work out what is different about them and therefore who they are. Reaching the last page, you will likely feel a strong urge to assert your own humanness: to shout, to dance, to make love. And why not?

Two more books about love for the month of May

The Paris Wife by Paula McLain (2011)

The best book in the world to give to someone who is ill in bed or some such, this is about the love affair between Hadley Hemingway and her husband, a writer you might have heard of named Ernest. Its themes include marriage, and gender, and genius, and writing, and Paris and Paris and Paris. I mean, who doesn't want to read endlessly about Paris? And that scene where Hadley leaves her husband's manuscript on the train! It also makes you immediately want to go out and read the non-fiction version, *Paris Without End: The True Story of Hemingway's First Wife* by Gioia Diliberto (2011), as well as take a squizz at Ernest's *The Sun Also Rises* (1926), if only to see what all the fuss is about.

A Little Life by Hanya Yanagihara (2015)

It might seem odd to recommend this novel in this context, because the narrative is at times horrifically violent and sad, but it is also often beautiful and healing, and its overarching theme is love. This is truly the best example I have ever come across in literature of the transformative power of the enduring love of friends and family. You are the person you were before you read this book, then the person you are afterwards – it will genuinely rearrange you just a fraction. Be prepared, though, for the wracking sobs that will emerge from you as you turn the last page. Straight-up devastating, unbelievably moving, strangely uplifting.

Top ten books about mothering

1/*Hamnet*
by Maggie O'Farrell (2020)
In which the only son of Anne Hathaway and William Shakespeare dies of the plague. Never have I cried so much reading a book...

2/*The Light Between Oceans*
by M L Stedman (2012)
...oh, hang on a minute, yes I have – it was this one, which is about a young couple living in a lighthouse off the coast of Australia when one day a dinghy washes up ashore with a baby girl inside it.

3/*The Blank Wall*
by Elisabeth Sanxay Holding (1947)
A thriller about a mother who will do anything to defend her daughter from a blackmailing boyfriend. Like a less boring Raymond Chandler.

4/*The Joys of Motherhood*
by Buchi Emecheta (1979)
An eye-opening insight into what it was like to be a mother in rural Nigeria in the middle of the 20th century. Unique in the true sense of the word.

5/*Olive Kitteridge* (2008) or
My Name is Lucy Barton (2016)
both by Elizabeth Strout
The first is so sad and true about sons, the second the same about daughters.

6/*Territory of Light*
by Yuko Tsushima (1979)
Life in a Tokyo flat for a divorced mother and her two-year-old. Fierce, fascinating, honest.

7/*Princes in the Land*
by Joanna Cannan (1938)
Sometimes, I am afraid, your children will end up disappointing you, as in this highly readable cautionary tale about an overbearing, snobbish mother living in Oxford in between the wars, who is forced to come to terms with the fact that none of her darlings are going to take the path in life she had hoped they might.

8/*The Perfect Nanny*

by Leïla Slimani (2016)
Set in Paris's 10th arrondissement, this is a terrifying novel about a relationship between a mother and a nanny that goes very, very wrong. Only to be read when feeling resilient.

9/*The Millstone*

by Margaret Drabble (1965)
An unmarried academic gets pregnant in 1960s London and is beset by woes. The book includes some haunting period details about the workings of the early NHS, such as the way that single mothers were called 'Mrs' rather than 'Miss' by the midwives and had to have a sign with the letter 'U' hanging from their hospital bed to denote their marital status.

10/*The Days of Abandonment*

by Elena Ferrante (2002)
A brutally honest account of one Italian mother's rage and despair at being stuck at home with two small children. It feels, at last, as if someone is telling the truth.

Timeline: A few highlights in modern science fiction *in case* Never Let Me Go *leaves you wanting more.*

1951 *The Day of the Triffids* by John Wyndham, in which everyday life in 1950s England takes a turn for the weird.

1961 In *Solaris*, amazing Polish writer Stanislaw Lem offers up one of the first literary attempts to imagine alien life. I love almost all forms of Polish cultural expression and this is no exception.

1979 *The Hitchhiker's Guide to the Galaxy* by Douglas Adams is a seminal text for comedy nerds, sci-fi nerds, and all the best sorts of nerds, in fact.

1984 Debuts do not come more seismic than William Gibson's cyberpunk masterpiece *Necromancer*. Not only did it redefine the entire genre of science fiction, but it established Gibson as perhaps its greatest living stylist. With a strung-out hacker for a hero, this seedy, smoggy, tactile novel made any other vision of the future look hopelessly uncool.

1993 *Parable of the Sower* by Octavia E Butler is set in a violent, anarchic, future Los Angeles, where civilization has almost completely collapsed and the climate crisis is a fact of life. So, maybe not so far in the future, after all.

1997 *Blindness* by José Saramoga is a haunting vision of a parallel world where suddenly everyone goes blind. Not an easy read.

2001 *Noughts and Crosses* by Malorie Blackman, a story in which black people oppress white, rather than the other way around. Highly original and thought-provoking, as well as a zippy read.

2015 *The Day the Sun Died* by Yan Lianke is narrated by a 14-year-old living in a hilltop village in China, and offers a satirical take on life under the Chinese Communist Party. It is unlike anything you have ever read.

2016 In Naomi Alderman's *The Power*, the women of the world discover they can vanquish men by releasing jolts of electricity out of their arms, allowing them to become the dominant gender. You'll never look at your arm in the same way again.

2020 *The Ministry for the Future* by Kim Stanley Robinson is an utterly terrifying novel about an organization set up by the Paris Agreement to lobby on behalf of those living on Earth in the future so that they can have as much say in developments as those living on Earth in the present. Some would call it climate fiction, I would call it horror fiction – anyway, it's some sort of fiction. At least, let's hope it's fiction.

January
February
March
April
May

June

July
August
September
October
November
December

What is one to say about June – the time of perfect
young summer, the fulfilment of the promise of
the earlier months, and with as yet no sign to
remind one that its fresh young beauty will ever
fade? For my own part I wander up into the wood
and say, 'June is here – June is here; thank God
for lovely June!

Gertrude Jekyll, *Wood and Garden* (1899)

*J*un, *juin, Juni, junio, giugno, litha, lipanj, czerwiec, Haziran:*
whatever your language of choice, June is a month of infinite
variety. The official gatekeeper to high summer, it is in June that
your diary starts to fill up just a little too much: weddings, anniversaries,
parties, it is often a whirlwind of fun and excitement. The last few
weeks of the academic year give way to the first adventures outdoors
in the forest or on the beach. Freedom beckons.

In the southern hemisphere, June plays host to the shortest day
of the year, and therefore the winter solstice; meanwhile, of course,
the northern hemisphere enjoys its longest day and, with it, the
summer solstice. The word 'solstice' comes from the Latin phrase
sol sistere, meaning 'sun stands still', and in many countries, especially
in Europe, it is a time of ecstatic traditional celebration. Bonfires are
built to scare off evil spirits that might ruin the harvest. In some
countries, it is a time to gather herbs and give thanks for the gift of
fertility; magical charms are thought to be at their strongest. In the
United Kingdom, druids convene at Stonehenge, while in Sweden
pickled herring is on the menu and flower crowns hit the height of

their popularity. This is a joyful time to give thanks for the long days, the harvest and family – in essence, to celebrate life.

In many countries, Father's Day is also on the third Sunday in June (except in Europe's Catholic countries, when it is on 19 March, which is St Joseph's Day). Personally, I aim to encourage my children to show their appreciation for their parents every day of the year, rather than just the one; for this reason we do not celebrate either Father's Day or Mother's Day in our house. This recently resulted in one of my sons composing the following inimitable lines of poetry in response to his teacher's insistence that he must make me a card:

This is a Mother's Day poem.
I know you don't really care.
But I am forced to,
While sitting in this chair.

I appreciate I am in the minority here, however, in my curmudgeonly approach to these kinds of holidays; perhaps a compromise would be to acknowledge these holidays through our choice of reading matter instead.

With this in mind, let us browse our bookshelves for texts that are fresh and different in terms of style or culture, helping us look at the world anew. There is a sense in June that life is whizzing by faster than ever. Thus, books set over the course of a single day suit the mood, allowing us to slow down just for a second. As the same time, let us look to the light, seeking out books that are full of surprises.

Ulysses

BY JAMES JOYCE (1922)

W hen I was 22, I spent the month of June travelling around the Balkans by myself. I was trying to heal a broken heart, having been unexpectedly dumped by a boyfriend. Night after night, I ate supper alone in a taverna with just my book for company. The book in question was not only one of the longest in the English language (which was lucky, because it easily lasted me the whole trip), but is also often perceived as one of the most difficult. But what else was I going to do? Re-read the *rakia* menu?

And this is what became clear to me over a series of seafood spaghetti dishes. *Ulysses* is one of the funniest books you will ever read, as well as the very definition of 'un-boring'. A silly, absurd, hilarious outpouring of all that is miraculous about the English language, the key is not to take it seriously, ever, in any way, at all. This is one reason why the book should be read during the most joyous of months, June, which always feels so marvellously full of potential. The other reason is that the entirety of *Ulysses* is set on a single day in June: on the 16th, to be precise, in 1904, which also happens to be when James Joyce first stepped out with his wife-to-be, Nora Barnacle.

James Joyce was born in Dublin in 1882, the eldest of ten children. He spent most of his adulthood living a precarious existence travelling between Paris, Zurich and Trieste with Nora and their two children, Giorgio and Lucia. He worked on *Ulysses* throughout the course of the First World War; it was published in 1922 on his 40th birthday.

Ulysses was inspired by the ancient Greek writer Homer's epic poem *The Odyssey*. Joyce changes the name of the wandering hero from Odysseus to Leopold Bloom, re-imagining him as an Irish Jew going about his ordinary day. At the same time, Joyce eschews literary convention in order to invent an entirely new way of expressing himself, mainly through putting streams of consciousness on paper. There are parallels to be found in the emergence of new forms of music such as rock 'n' roll or grime: it is still music, but unlike anything that has gone before. The way to read *Ulysses*, therefore, is to come at the text more for the general feel of it than the specifics of plot or character. For *Ulysses* offers the ultimate expression of the power and beauty of the English language; to seek out narrative is somewhat to miss the point.

It is thus entirely permissible and even sensible to skip some bits of *Ulysses*. In a way, that is its wonder: structured into 18 'episodes', each differs hugely from the others, including in terms of appeal and accessibility. It opens in a jolly fashion as two young men, Buck Mulligan and Stephen Dedalus, chat, argue and scoff breakfast, building beautifully to Episode 4, which draws the reader in with its glorious description of Bloom's breakfast, then zips along around the streets of Dublin until we meet Bloom's wife Molly, who is still in bed and thinking about her lover.

The best episodes? Well, I adore Episode 14 for the silliness of its language, especially towards the end when Leopold is in the pub getting roaringly drunk: 'Come on, you winefizzling ginsizzling booseguzzling existences!' is how I, too, persuade my friends to hurry up and finish their drinks before the chip shop closes. Episode 17, meanwhile, is an exquisite feat of linguistic invention: Leopold muses on everything from the advantages of shaving at nighttime to what he admires most about water. It is verbose, overblown and ridiculous, and I love it with a passion.

But it is the last episode in the book, Episode 18, that will always be closest to my heart. The reader is invited to eavesdrop on Molly Bloom's interior monologue as she lies in bed next to her husband. The writing style closely mimics Nora Joyce's in her letters to her husband, in particular the unpunctuated meandering of passionate feeling as well as the unsurpassable turn of phrase, for example her mockery of an erect penis as 'sticking up at you like a hatrack'. Molly also illustrates more vividly than almost any of the other characters what is, in my view, the central theme of *Ulysses*: the heroism in the everyday. Just getting through is enough, right?

Miss Pettigrew Lives for a Day

BY WINIFRED WATSON (1938)

*M*iss Pettigrew Lives for a Day was an immediate hit when it first came out in 1938, but six books later, in 1943, its Newcastle-based author Winifred Watson stopped writing forever. She later claimed that it was because 'There are only six things in life you can write about and then you've said everything,' but it was surely no coincidence that she had also just had a baby. Sigh: as Virginia Woolf so memorably put it, 'How any woman with a family ever put pen to paper, I cannot fathom. Always the bell rings and the baker calls.' Indeed.

Miss Pettigrew Lives for a Day is the book for which the word 'charming' was invented. The closest comparison is to a rainbow, or perhaps a meringue: it is something to clutch to your soul and adore. Equally, it is a celebration of life's wonderful potential. You simply never know what the next day will bring.

The plot, it must be said, is slim. Guinevere Pettigrew is 40 years old and has led a drab existence as a not-very-good governess. Terrorized both by the harassed mothers and the naughty children, she confronts destitution. The only bright spot in her life is going to the cinema once a week. *Miss Pettigrew Lives for a Day* vividly conveys the difficulties faced by some women who didn't manage to catch a man to look after them (one of the 'surplus women' of the

1920s) and whose only recourse if she could not stay at home with her parents was to become a governess or companion.

On arrival at 5 Onslow Mansions, Miss Pettigrew assumes the employment agency has sent her to look after some unruly charges; instead, it is the beautiful and charismatic Delysia Lafosse who opens the door and welcomes her in as a cross between the housekeeper and friend Delysia desperately needs. And so Miss Pettigrew's day begins: like *Ulysses*, it takes place over the course of 24 hours, during which Miss Pettigrew sees off an annoying suitor, rescues Delysia from various disasters, and accompanies her on her (mostly slightly insalubrious) adventures.

Miss Pettigrew Lives for a Day is delightfully funny, splendidly uplifting and slyly elliptical: at one point Miss Pettigrew enquires how Delysia's friend Miss Dubarry came to own a beauty parlour. 'Oh, that', Miss Dubarry replies. 'That was very simple. I vamped the boss... I was eighteen... an apprentice. He was getting on. They always fall for the young ones... He got a nice tombstone and I got the parlour.' *Miss Pettigrew Lives for a Day* is in some ways the literary equivalent of the Billy Wilder film, *Some Like it Hot*. A classic. A treasure. A treat.

From the idiosyncratic chapter headings (Chapter Four 12.52 pm–1.17pm; Chapter Ten 7.52 pm–8.52 pm) to the perfect contemporary line drawings by Mary Thomson (my favourite is the one captioned simply, 'Cocaine?'), this sweet, naughty book is truly like no other. It is for happy days (Miss Pettigrew and the cigar butts), for sad days (Joe in the taxi) and everything in between. It is the best book for anyone who is feeling a little low, or broken-hearted, or convalescing; it will cheer them up no end.

Two texts that help us look at the world anew

The Enlightenment of the Greengage Tree
by Shokoofeh Azar (2017)

Originally written in Farsi, this is Azar's first novel to be translated into English. It is a stunning, memorable, moving account of one family's life in post-1979 revolutionary Iran. The twist is that the narrator of this brilliant book is dead – the ghost, to be precise, of a 13-year-old girl killed in a fire caused by revolutionaries burning down her father's tar (a traditional musical instrument) workshop. However, in a beautifully realized and plausible manner, being a ghost does not stop her being part of the family. Steeped in tragedy (a rudimentary knowledge of 20th-century Iranian history is useful here, but by no means essential) with an undoubtedly melancholy tone (a sense of loss pervades the book throughout – both of people and of a culture seemingly lost forever), the book manages, nevertheless, to be uplifting, funny and wise. Azar has a real talent for narrative prose; the result is a work of great beauty.

Also
Try

Americanah
by Chimamanda Ngozi Adichie (2013)

Like the month of June, this widely adored novel about Ifemelu and Obinze, two childhood sweethearts who meet at school in Nigeria then go their separate ways to America and England, has a lot going on. Adichie is endlessly entertaining in the way she spools out the highly involving plot, interwoven with her characteristically witty, acerbic commentary on issues of race, class and culture. Take, for instance, her description of the kind of books that Ifemelu's boyfriend recommends to her: 'novels by young and youngish men and packed with things, a fascinating, confounding accumulation of brands and music and comic books and icons, with emotions skimmed over, and each sentence stylishly aware of its own stylishness...' Adichie has described *Americanah* as 'an unapologetic love story' and she's not wrong, adding 'Don't we all in the end write about love? All literature is about love.' Which is an incredibly interesting statement to ponder.

Top ten fresh and different books about the migrant experience *for those who loved* Americanah

1/*The Lonely Londoners*
by Samuel Selvon (1956)
This slim, enticing, groundbreaking novel about Caribbean immigrants in London in the 1950s, written contemporaneously, is a huge favourite of mine.

2/*What Is The What*
by Dave Eggers (2006)
This novel about a Sudanese child soldier who settles in America is a surprisingly charming work of witness. I say 'novel': it is really a fictionalized autobiography, but I think that still counts.

3/*The Emigrants*
by W G Sebald (1992)
A hybrid of fiction and non-fiction, Sebald explores the experience of four different emigrants from Germany in the aftermath of the Second World War in this innovative, imaginative musing on the meaning of foreignness.

4/*The Luminaries*
by Eleanor Catton (2013)
Set on New Zealand's South Island during the gold rush of the mid-19th century, this is a ripping, gripping tale of murder and opium and gold and shipping and banking. Reads a bit like a Dickens novel, but with more of a Maori presence.

5/*Homegoing*
by Yaa Gyasi (2016)
I could not stop thinking about this book for days after I had finished it. The lives of two half-sisters in Ghana diverge dramatically after one is captured and sold to British slave traders, but the other remains in the village where they were born. The scale of the narrative is huge while at the same time managing to tell a small and intimate story about how we establish a sense of belonging in an ever-changing world.

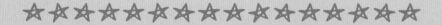

6/Incomparable World
by S I Martin (1996)
African–American soldiers arrive in London in the years immediately after the American Revolution. Discover this alternative perspective of what it is like to be the new kid in town.

7/Brick Lane
by Monica Ali (2003)
An engrossing and funny debut novel about an 18-year-old woman from Bangladesh who finds herself married off to an older man and living in a high-rise block in East London. It is so visceral that it captures the delicious smell of curry just right.

8/Pachinko
by Min Jin Lee (2017)
I am very fond of this instantly immersive novel about a Korean family that emigrates to Japan at the beginning of the 20th century. Ideal for those planning to sneak in an early summer holiday, it is a fabulous beach read in the best possible sense.

9/My Ántonia
by Willa Cather (1918)
Members of a Czech immigrant family find themselves struggling to make a life on a homestead in Nebraska (where Cather herself grew up) at the end of the 19th century. A vivid recreation of frontier life that puts a young working-class woman at the centre of the story in a radical act of literary subversiveness.

10/Exit West
by Mohsin Hamid (2017)
Set in a near-future dystopia, this is a mildly-experimental-but-not-in-a-scary-way novel about a young couple who use a series of magical doors to flee a civil war and end up in a refugee camp, then London, then California. An interesting and timely take on what it means to be a refugee.

Top ten books with an interesting perspective on fatherhood in *celebration of Father's Day*

1/*Daddy Was a Number Runner*
by Louise Meriwether (1970)
Set in Harlem in the 1930s, 12-year-old Francie sees her father unable to find legal work and thus forced into becoming a number runner, collecting people's numbers as part of an underground gambling racket in the days before legal lotteries existed. Meriwether is a genius at characterization; this is a brave, rare account of African–American life above 110th Street.

2/*Le Père Goriot*
by Honoré de Balzac (1834)
'Don't love your daughters too much or it will end up destroying you' seems to be the moral of this classic tale set in Paris in 1819. One of the earliest realist novels, its detailed, evocative descriptions of people's houses, meals and clothes, as well as the accounts of ongoing tussles for social status, were ground-breaking at the time. If this feels like slightly hard work for the first few pages, stick with it and you will be rewarded.

3/*Gilead*
by Marilynne Robinson (2004)
A story of fathers and sons that has very much its own vibe. Set in Gilead in Iowa in 1956, narrated by 76-year-old Reverend John Ames, this is a deeply serious book – a spiritual one, even – but not a po-faced one. It is like a calming Sunday morning in church with the handsomest boy in the village sitting in the aisle across from you.

4/*A House for Mr Biswas*
by V S Naipaul (1961)
Inspired by the author's own father, this is the tale of the son of an impoverished labourer in Trinidad who is forced to live with his in-laws, besides various other indignities. He gets work as a sign painter, then opens a dry goods store, then briefly becomes a journalist, but always seems to end up pretty much back where he started. A fascinating look at life in Trinidad in the early 20th century, as well as the struggles of trying to be a good family man.

5/Pride and Prejudice

by Jane Austen (1813)
Mr Bennett is one of the most famous fathers in literature, boasting an endlessly quotable turn of phrase, for example: 'For what do we live, but to make sport for our neighbors, and laugh at them in our turn.' Usually to be found hiding in his library and wondering after his favourite daughter (Elizabeth, obviously), his kindness and amusement have been a delight for generations of readers to behold, no matter how much he pretends to be cantankerous.

6/My Struggle

by Karl Ove Knausgaard (2009)
I thought this series of six novels was as dull as ditchwater, but I appreciate I am in the minority and books one and six in particular do offer an unusually intimate portrayal of fatherhood.

7/About a Boy

by Nick Hornby (1998)
A super-cute novel about, well, a boy. And a man. And their relationship. Touching and true.

8/The Chosen

by Chaim Potok (1967)
The first American novel about the modern Jewish Orthodox community. Set in Williamsburg in Brooklyn in the 1940s, it is about two boys, Reuven and Danny, who attend different yeshivas but meet playing softball. Potok tracks each boy's differing relationship with his strictly observant father to moving effect.

9/On Beauty

by Zadie Smith (2005)
Howards End begins with letters from Helen to her sister; this homage to Howards End begins with a series of emails from Jerome to his father, a university professor. Smith shines brightly in whatever she writes, and this is no exception.

10/Wonder

by R J Palacio (2012)
Originally written as YA (young adult) fiction, the dad in this beautiful book struggles in a very human way when his son is bullied for having a rare craniofacial disorder, emerging a hero of kindness and tolerance.

January
February
March
April
May
June

July

August
September
October
November
December

Summer afternoon – summer afternoon; to me,
those have always been the two most beautiful
words in the English language.

Henry James, as recalled by Edith Wharton in
***A Backward Glance* (1934)**

I n many countries, summer is at its best in July – not like the final furious heat of August, but not like the nervy and changeable start of June, either. Warm nights and even warmer days combine with the beginning of the school holidays, which seem to change the energy in the air whether you are still a pupil or not, to create a joyous sense of potential.

Most of the world now follows the Gregorian calendar, introduced by Pope Gregory XIII in 1582, but the ancient Roman calendar remains the source for many of the names of the months and July, honouring Julius Caesar, is no exception. However, the Roman influence does not end there. The Latin term *dies caniculares*, from which the English phrase 'dog days' derives, refers to the time of year when the brightest star in the sky, the dog star Sirius, first becomes visible in the east again. 'Dog days' has now come to mean the hottest and most humid days of the summer – that is, when lying around in a hammock reading a book is the only order of the day.

What you need is a guaranteed good read – the most important component of which is, in my view, having a very strong plot (many that pretend to have a strong plot really don't). 'I couldn't put it down', you will tell your friends, which in some ways is perhaps the highest possible compliment you can pay a book.

A LITTLE SUMMER INTERLUDE

'It was one of those midsummer Sundays when everyone sits around saying, "I drank too much".' This is the opening sentence of the short story 'The Swimmer' by John Cheever (1964), in which a young man named Neddy Merrill sits by his friend's pool, *'one hand in it, one around a glass of gin'*, when he has the idea to try to swim all the way home via the kind of river of swimming pools that exists in the neighborhood. He sets off, but before long the pools get chillier, everyone seems less friendly and a storm looms. At the same time as he swims, even though it is still afternoon, there are signs that the season is changing from summer to autumn while, in parallel, his own sense of self begins to disappear amongst all the confusion. Darkness falls both outside of him and inside of him. This highly atmospheric short story is an exquisitely realized blend of realism and surrealism and precisely the right length to keep you occupied while you're waiting for the barbecue to heat up or the sun to come out from behind a cloud.

City of Girls

BY ELIZABETH GILBERT (2019)

The fact that this novel is set in the world of showgirls in 1940s Manhattan should be enough to recommend it alone. I'll be honest: it does not feature the most brilliantly constructed sentences or structural flourishes and I give you full permission to skip the first chapter, which is a bit pedestrian and does not quite ring true, BUT all this is forgiven in an instant once you immerse yourself in the rest of the novel, which is so jolly, and sexy, and fun – the mostest of the most.

The novel opens with 19-year-old Vivian dropping out of Vassar: 'I spent the first two weeks of June hitting a tennis ball against the side of our garage while whistling "Little Brown Jug" again and again, until finally my parents got sick of me and shipped me off to live with my aunt in the city, and honestly, who could blame them?' Luckily, her aunt is Aunt Peg, who runs a theatre in midtown Manhattan. Vivian joins the family business, becomes a showgirl, and what larks ensue!

'Our chosen line of work that summer was romping and rampaging,' Vivian recalls of that heady time spent in the giddy world of interwar New York, with a cast of splendidly drawn characters – her glamorous partner-in-crime Celia, her handsome dalliance and co-star Anthony, Hollywood wheeler-dealer Billy Buell – to educate her in the ways of the world and introduce her to love, lust and drinking gin fizzes 'until we forgot how to walk.' Any novel that references gin fizzes is a hit with me, for sure.

Gilbert is a consistently witty observer of human behaviour, for instance: 'He and I had been talking about jazz (which is to say that he had been talking about jazz, and I had been listening to him talk about jazz, because that is how you talk to a man about jazz)...' She is especially perceptive, however, on the subject of female sexuality. When Vivian reaches her 40s, a little hardened and heartbroken, she comes to the realization that, in truth, her great love is sex: 'at some point in a woman's life, she just gets tired of being ashamed all the time. After that, she is free to become whoever she truly is.' Whether you agree or not, it is an unusual and interesting perspective, reminding us that attitudes towards female sexual freedom have perhaps not moved on as much as we might think. Gilbert once explained that she felt compelled to write *City of Girls* because 'there was something missing in the Western canon of literature: a story about women with really active sex lives whose lives are not destroyed by it.' In other words, it is OK to seek sexual pleasure without ending up dead like Anna Karenina, Madame Bovary or Effi Briest (all of whom are characters written by men, of course).

If Elizabeth Gilbert's most famous book *Eat, Pray, Love* (2006) was not for you (as it certainly was not for me), please don't let that put you off. She once said she wanted *City of Girls* to 'go down like a champagne cocktail – light and bright, crisp and fun' and it does start out like this, but as each chapter passes, a better analogy would be something with far more depth: a pisco sour, perhaps, or even a Manhattan. By the end, you will marvel at Gilbert's profundity, yet always with a light touch, about women and relationships and, well, LIFE. She is particularly brilliant on the subject of female friendship: how, in some ways, friendship is really the greatest form of love. No wonder *City of Girls* is the book I give to my friends if they are ill, or sad, or in a reading rut brought on by a global pandemic – it is a sure-fire winner every time.

Top ten *sure-fire, guaranteed, money-back-if-I'm wrong,* **'good reads'**

1/*The Vanishing Half*
by Brit Bennett (2020)

2/*A Man Called Ove*
by Fredrik Backman (2012)

3/The Cazalet Chronicles
by Elizabeth Jane Howard (1990–2013)

4/*Older Brother*
by Mahir Guven (2017)

5/*Queenie*
by Candice Carty-Williams (2019)

6/*The Teleportation Accident*
by Ned Beauman (2012)

7/*Tipping the Velvet*
by Sarah Waters (1998)

8/*The Underground Railroad*
by Colson Whitehead (2016)

9/*The Party*
by Elizabeth Day (2017)

10/*Life After Life*
by Kate Atkinson (2013)

Ghost Wall

BY SARAH MOSS (2018)

L et's talk about Gothic fiction, which is currently experiencing something of a revival thanks to the likes of Sarah Perry, Andrew Michael Hurley and, in particular, Sarah Moss. Gothic fiction allows us to deal with our darkest fears, in part by leaving space for the strange and the peculiar – a refreshing rebellion against trying to explain the unexplainable. Sarah Moss's sixth novel, *Ghost Wall*, encapsulates all this and more. It is 150 pages of stark prose that veers from beauty to horror and back again.

Sarah Moss is a novelist and academic who also teaches creative writing – and, gosh, does she have a lot to say. Set in mid-July, *Ghost Wall* is a powerful rendering of one summer that teenager Sylvie spends in the shadow of Hadrian's Wall with her mum, her dad and a group of archaeology students. The idea is to try to recreate Iron Age life as closely as possible.

This short, sharp novel starts off gently: 'The day was bright again, as if England had forgotten how to rain.' Sylvie follows her father's instructions to forage for garlic greens and wild thyme, but to her shock (and also awe) some of the other students accompanying her sneak off to the corner shop and buy sweets. The lighter-hearted side of this book vividly recreates the experience of a terrible camping holiday: the sleepless nights, suppers that take hours to cook, trips to the loo in the middle of the night trying not to trip over a tree.

It quickly becomes clear, however, that Sylvie and her mother are under the coercive control of Sylvie's tyrannical father. As she wrestles with the campfire, trying to make gruel for breakfast, the two women discuss how 'It wasn't fair for Dad to tell us off for oversleeping when he'd made us leave our watches at home and kept talking about the benefits of life without clocks. Folks lived by their bellies and the sun, then, weren't forever counting off the minutes, folk knew patience in the old days'. The novel raises the question of whether the 'old days' really were better, or just better for oppressing women. After a brutal and troubling incident where Sylvie's father skins a rabbit with excessive glee, the rest of the group begin to realize that there are dark undertones to his project.

The narrative of *Ghost Wall* centres on the bog people: Iron Age residents of the borderlands who were buried in peat thousands of years ago and thus naturally mummified. Sylvie's father explains how one particular bog girl was most likely murdered by a blow to the head. 'Yes, I said, I see. Her hands had been bound for two thousand years', is Sylvie's quietly terrified response. Moss ends the paragraph here to devastating effect, allowing the reader a moment to re-read the line, take a breath, acknowledge the horror contained within it, and keep reading, one's heart beating just a little bit more frantically than before.

Moss has said that she likes books 'that are not "relatable" to me, books that are windows more than mirrors'. And *Ghost Wall* is exactly that: through the unlikely lens of the bog people, she provides a wholly new perspective on modern life. We see our 'shared world from places other than our own and through eyes other than our own'. Moss places contemporary misogyny in the context of Iron Age rituals and beliefs, exploring the way young women have been treated by societies past and present. The reader is quick to realize that, at its heart, this is a novel about violence against women.

Ghost Wall is told entirely in the first person from Sylvie's point of view. The sentences are long, as are the paragraphs, and there is

minimal punctuation. Yet such is Moss's skill that the text is never confusing or alienating. 'Precise' would be the word that describes her style most accurately. And you will never, ever forget the penultimate scene, which includes a sentence that made me gasp louder than I have ever gasped before. You are going to have to read the book, though, to find out what it is.

SUMMER LOVE

We can't possibly have a summer love. So many people have tried that the name's become proverbial. Summer is only the unfulfilled promise of spring, a charlatan in place of the warm balmy nights I dream of in April. It's a sad season of life without growth...It has no day.

F. Scott Fitzgerald,
This Side of Paradise (1920)

Dorothy Whipple
The ultimate 'good read'

Born Dorothy Stirrup in Blackburn, England, in 1893, this most under-recognized of under-recognized authors had her heart broken at an early age, when her close friend George Owen was killed in week one of the First World War. She subsequently went to work as a secretary to Henry Whipple, a widower 24 years her senior, and after three years of typing and filing she married him.

Having settled in Nottingham, Whipple proceeded to write eight highly successful novels. Every single one is the very definition of a 'good read'. Her recurring themes include family, marriage, the home, life generally in the 20th century and often in the north of England; she consistently constructs a story that is seemingly entirely ordinary, but the plotting and characterization is so highly skilled, every sentence so magnificently written, that it is a mystery why she is not better known.

Focus on...

My favourite Whipple novels are *They Were Sisters* (1943), *Someone at a Distance* (1953) and *The Priory* (1939), but honestly they are all wonderful. Some, like *High Wages* (1930), are quite light-hearted, whereas others, such as *They Knew Mr Knight* (1934), are more serious and disturbing, but not a single one disappoints. You really are in for a treat if you haven't yet discovered this truly marvellous novelist.

Two books that smell of sunshine

The Shape of Water by Andrea Camilleri (1994)

The first in a series of Italian police procedural novels about a detective named Inspector Montelbano, translated into English by poet Stephen Sartarelli, this is to be read with an Aperol spritz in your hand while perspiring mildly. It is terrifically evocative of life in contemporary Sicily; almost every breakthrough is followed by a meal of some sort, such as the casual weekday supper of spaghetti with a sauce of sea urchin pulp that Montalbano rustles up one afternoon following a dip in the sea. Further on in the book, he variously devours red peppers straight from the fridge, tries out a new recipe for baby octopus and makes a friend some pasta with garlic and oil. Highly Italian, highly entertaining.

Also Try

Middlesex by Jeffrey Eugenides (2002)

This is such a nourishing book: massively, joyously fun but simultaneously profound. Beginning in a grandmother's silkworm cocoonery in a tiny village overlooking Mount Olympus, it is about three generations of a Greek–American family but with a particular focus on Cali, who discovers they are a hermaphrodite. The word 'hermaphrodite' derives from the Greek mythological figure Hermaphrodite, who was the child of Aphrodite and Hermes and existed as both male and female at the same time. The novel places being intersex in historical context and is fascinating about the phenomenon generally. This is the very best kind of beach read: a deliciously long epic in which you can immerse yourself for days without feeling guilty that you are not seeing the sights or earning your PADI certificate.

January
February
March
April
May
June
July
August
September
October
November
December

*Today is the first of August. It is hot, steamy
and wet. It is raining. I am tempted to write
a poem. But I remember what it said on one
rejection slip: After a heavy rainfall, poems
titled RAIN pour in from across the nation.*

The Journals of Sylvia Plath, August 1950

Augugust is summer's grand finale. Traditionally the month when normal life is put on 'pause' while everyone goes on holiday, it has an edge to it that July does not: sweatier, angrier, fiercer. Perhaps because of the heat?

August boasts more meteor showers than any other month: the Kappa Cygnids reliably make an appearance, more often than not accompanied by the likes of Alpha Capricornids, the Perseids, and the Southern Delta Aquariids around the same time. To add to the drama, this is not even the only natural phenomenon to demand attention, with two famous volcanic eruptions occurring in this month: Krakatoa (26 August, 1883) and Pompei (24 August, 79 CE).

The long summer nights encourage the sense that this is a highly-charged month when anything can happen. Passionate affairs, angry riots, sweaty parties: humanity is at its most visceral as everyone tries their best to avoid *la rentrée*, as the French call it, or the return to real life. It is also indisputably the sexiest of months – again, I suppose, because of the heat. Let's strive to have our reading reflect this. We want books that are accessible enough to read on the beach, yet match the intensity of the season. *On y va!*

Neapolitan Quartet

BY ELENA FERRANTE (2011–14, FIRST ENGLISH TRANSLATION 2012–15 BY ANN GOLDSTEIN)

I am going to break all the rules here and recommend four books instead of one, but you don't mind, do you? After all, Ferrante herself breaks the rules all the time and I want to be just like her when I grow up (anonymous, living in Naples, internationally lauded...). Hopefully in August you will have time on your hands to power your way through this life-changing series of literary magic. Am I being over the top? I don't care. Ferrante deserves it. Her writing is also eminently suited to reading in August: sweaty, sultry, hot-headed and always with a bit of an edge.

The name Elena Ferrante is a pseudonym. Almost all we know for sure about the author of the Neapolitan quartet is that she was born in Naples, writes books and is married with children. Frankly, I have no interest in knowing more. It does not matter to me who she is, or where she lives, or who she's married to. What matters to me is the writing.

The first book in the quartet is titled *My Brilliant Friend*. It is about a friendship between two girls, Elena and Lila, in a working-class neighbourhood in Naples, Italy, in the 1950s. They meet when they are six: Elena's father is a porter at city hall and Lila's father is a shoemaker, while their mothers cook and clean and rage. Both girls are desperately clever, which turns out to be equally a blessing and a burden. *My Brilliant Friend* is wonderful, but even more wonderful in my view are the second and third books in the quartet: *The Story of a New Name* and *Those Who Leave and Those Who Stay*.

Ferrante captures better than anyone else the essence of what it is to be a woman. In particular, she writes about female rage in a truly revelatory way, drawing attention to the exhausting combination of oppression, drudgery, sexual harassment and loss of identity that many women face as they move through the world. These novels are not kind to the male sex, for sure, highlighting the daily violence that was a feature of Naples' extremely patriarchal society. Take the way fathers casually hit their children, in one instance sending Lila flying out of a window, leaving her with a broken arm, and yet it is barely commented upon because it is seen as totally normal. In other words, women are right to be angry; they have a lot to be angry about. And yet, sometimes, it becomes anger of such force that it has the potential to destroy everything and everyone around it, a little like a volcano erupting.

Ferrante frequently returns to the concept of *frantumaglia*, which she explains as 'a jumble of fragments...the word for a disquiet not otherwise definable, it referred to a miscellaneous crowd of things in her head, debris in a muddy water of the brain'. It is a discombobulated state shared by Lila, Elena and a number of other female characters across the quartet; Ferrante seems to suggest that this is a result of the women simultaneously maintaining multiple roles for themselves (mothers, daughters, wives, workers, lovers) while keeping their true feelings, opinions and ambitions hidden away inside themselves. Certainly, her books are a vision of the world unashamedly from women's point of view. What she is offering is a dramatic shift in the centre of literary gravity.

Ferrante's writing is fierce, fearless and intense at every turn of the page, and I adore it with a passion. And with that said, I'm off to go and punch a wall then kiss a waiter.

AUGUST MUSINGS

There is no month in the whole year, in which nature wears a more beautiful appearance than in the month of August...Orchards and corn-fields ring with the hum of labour; trees bend beneath the thick clusters of rich fruit which bow their branches to the ground; and the corn, piled in graceful sheaves, or waving in every light breath that sweeps above it, as if it wooed the sickle, tinges the landscape with a golden hue. A mellow softness appears to hang over the whole earth...

Charles Dickens,
The Pickwick Papers (1836)

Persepolis

BY MARJANE SATRAPI (2000, FIRST ENGLISH
TRANSLATION 2003 BY MATTIAS RIPA)

I f you have not read a graphic novel before, let *Persepolis* be
where you start. It is accessible enough to read on the beach or
by the pool, but substantive and moving enough to make you feel
that you have not lost your critical faculties entirely as a result of too
many piña coladas and humid, sleepless nights.

Marjane Satrapi was born in Tehran, Iran, in 1969, into a middle-
class, politically active family, but moved to France as an adult, where
she spent many years working on *Persepolis* in an effort to make
sense of her complicated childhood. The book is a memoir in the form
of a graphic novel about life during the Iranian Revolution. If you just
read that sentence and had to admit to yourself that you are a bit hazy
on the details of the Iranian Revolution, especially how it impacted
families on a day-to-day basis, then that is at least one reason why
this book is for you.

Satrapi's fascinating first-person account of what it was like living
through these turbulent times opens with the overthrow of the Shah
in 1979. This is followed by the banning of the veil in 1980: 'I really
didn't know what to think about the veil. Deep down I was very
religious but as a family we were very modern and avant-garde.' She
remembers a game she used to play in the playground called
'Revolutionary' in which each child would assume a different role out

of Che Guevara, Fidel Castro, Trotsky and Lenin. It is a glimpse into what it is like to grow up in a family of revolutionaries, struggling against everyday injustices such as being censured for buying a Kim Wilde tape (the height of Western glamour at the time). In these accounts of daily life, Satrapi brings a human perspective to a nation too often associated with extremists (as she notes in the book's preface).

Persepolis is very funny in parts, for example when Satrapi explains to her grandma that she wants to be a prophet when she grows up so that she could help her grandma with her achy knees. It is also at times hauntingly sad. In one scene, she hears that her grandpa has been forced into a prison cell filled with water for hours at a time in an attempt to torture information out of him. To try to understand what he went through, she stays in the bath for an entire night. Through these unfiltered childish reactions and matter-of-fact accounts of the realities of life in such politically unstable times, the reader is offered a unique insight into 20th-century Iranian politics through the eyes of a ten-year-old.

When I finished *Persepolis*, I was struck by the absurdity of it having taken me so long to discover graphic novels. Please don't make the same mistake. *Persepolis* is a great gateway into the world of this genre. Continue your journey with an early classic like *Maus* by Art Spiegelman (1986), about the Holocaust, or a more recent gem like *Grass* by Keum Suk Gendry-Kim (2019), about a Korean girl forced into sexual slavery by the Japanese army during the Second World War. Their genius is to engage an additional area of the brain to a conventional novel, keeping it busy decoding the pictures at the same time as the words.

A few favourite books about the heat of desire

The Signature of All Things
by Elizabeth Gilbert (2013)
An excellent, clever read set in 19th-century Philadelphia that features, among other scenes that explore the parameters of female sexuality, an extraordinary scene of a 'no-touch' orgasm. Google it, it's a thing.

To Bed with Grand Music
by Marghanita Laski (1946)
Deborah says a tearful farewell to her husband as he goes off to fight in the Second World War, sits around and sews for a little while, then thinks 'sod this', moves to London and has sex with loads of men. An entirely different vision of women's wartime experiences to the ones we usually read about, and very refreshing for it.

Adèle
by Leila Slimani (2014)
A memorable French novel about a woman who leaves her husband in bed at night to go and have sex with random strangers she sees on the train. Not for the faint of heart.

Conversations with Friends
by Sally Rooney (2017)
A more contemporary-than-contemporary take on sex and sexuality set among college students in Dublin.

Little Children
by Tom Perrotta (2004)
The scene where two acquaintances from the playground have sex on the washing machine while the children nap is genuinely unforgettable. It has the potential to feature in your fantasies for many a child-bearing year to come.

The Pure and the Impure
by Colette (1932)
An odd, of-its-time, but fascinating meditation on the nature of sexual desire.

The Group
by Mary McCarthy (1963)
Eight Vassar graduates navigate life in New York City in this 1960s classic that was far head of its time. I promise you will never forget the scene where Dottie goes to the doctor to be fitted with a diaphragm.

Two books set amid intense heat

In Our Mad and Furious City by Guy Gunaratne (2019)

I am crazy about this debut novel. Capturing voices you feel you have not heard before and set in a world you feel you have not read about before, the action takes place over the course of a couple of days one recent, sweaty summer on a council estate in Neasden, north-west London. Five different characters narrate the story of how a British soldier has been killed and there is anger in the air: 'Fury was a fearsome drum, some hungry and hot temper, ill-spirit or madness that never touched us for long but followed our bodies for time.' Gunaratne is highly attuned to the language of the Neasden streets: enervating, fascinating, gorgeous in its joyousness and energy, brilliantly examining themes of gender, race and radicalism as the warm, urban sun beats down on the pavements.

Also Try

Midnight's Children by Salman Rushdie (1981)

A reading experience that is rather like an actual visit to India: over the top, overwhelming, almost too much – and yet also the most amazing time of your life. The book opens at midnight on 15 August 1948, as Saleem Sinai is born 'at the precise instant of India's arrival at independence'. Saleem's story becomes independent India's story. Set mostly in Bombay, everything he does is somehow reflected in national events, sometimes to a highly comic, even surreal, degree. One of Rushdie's earlier magic realist novels, *Midnight's Children* could not be richer in language: dense and intense, full of comic asides, a world of wonder and excitement and strangeness in the best possible sense. At its heart a family saga, it also manages to capture a broad sweep of Indian life, including the immediate aftermath of colonialism: 1947 was the year that a 'soldier's knife...cut a subcontinent in three'. I honestly don't know how you can not enjoy this book; I think it might actually be impossible.

Top ten books set in summer
(to be read on the days where the rain comes in and the summer holiday fast becomes a wash out...)

1/To the Lighthouse
by Virginia Woolf (1927)
The Ramsey family visit their summer home on the Isle of Skye in the modernist novel that changed everything...

2/The Virgin Suicides
by Jeffrey Eugenides (1993)
Set in Michigan in the 1970s, the summer heat engulfs five teenage sisters in tragedy; the boys in the neighborhood spend the rest of their lives trying to figure out what happened and why. The narrative oozes sweat on every page.

3/Lost Children Archive
by Valeria Luiselli (2019)
A mother and father set out on a road trip with their two kids, driving from New York City to Arizona, intent on documenting the migrant crisis at the Mexican–American border. An engaging, original, compassionate work of wonder.

4/A Room with a View
by E M Forster (1908)
Lucy Honeychurch gets kissed in a field of violets in the Italian countryside. Yes, please.

5/Sag Harbor
by Colson Whitehead (2009)
Benji, a monied African–American teenager, heads to his family's beach house in the Hamptons for the summer. A riveting novel touching on issues of class, race and ice cream.

6/The Interestings
by Meg Wolitzer (2013)
Tracing what happens in the years after six teenagers meet at summer camp in July 1974, this is an exploration of the sense of disappointment that so often pervades grown-up life, where no one is ever quite as successful or happy as they thought they would be.

7/*The Sun Also Rises*
by Ernest Hemingway (1926)
American and British expatriates travel from Paris to Pamplona to watch the running of the bulls and the bullfights. Sexy, cool, classic – like a man in a neckerchief and aviators.

8/*Outline*
by Rachel Cusk (2014)
An odd, original, literary novel about a woman teaching a writing course one very hot summer in Athens. Not an easy read, but definitely a rewarding one.

9/*Out Stealing Horses*
by Per Petterson (2003)
One summer in 1948, a 15-year-old boy visiting the Norwegian countryside near the Swedish border is persuaded by a friend to sneak into a field and steal some horses, along the way examining the sad aftermath of the Second World War.

10/*Summer*
by Edith Wharton (1917)
A 17-year-old girl's sexual awakening one summer in rural Massachusetts when a sexy young architect from the city comes to visit. Written after *The House of Mirth* and before *The Age of Innocence* and rather racy by Wharton's standards, but all the more thrilling for it.

January
February
March
April
May
June
July
August

September

October
November
December

*That old September feeling, left over from school
days, of summer passing, vacation nearly done,
obligations gathering, books and football in the
air...Another fall, another turned page: there was
something of jubilee in that annual autumnal
beginning, as if last year's mistakes had been
wiped clean by summer.*

Wallace Stegner, *Angle of Repose* (1971)

September features in the titles of more books than any other month: *The Last September* by Elizabeth Bowen (1929), good; *September* by Rosamunde Pilcher (1990), quite good; *The Septembers of Shiraz* by Dalia Sofer (2007), excellent; and more. I wonder why?

Perhaps it is because September has such a distinct atmosphere. For many of us it signifies the beginning of another academic year. Even as an adult, it is difficult to shake the overwhelming feeling of *la rentrée*. There is a sense of new beginnings; it feels like the moment to seek out some fresh perspective on the world.

From the *Mayflower* setting sail from Plymouth in 1620 to Handel finally finishing his *Messiah* in 1741 to the outbreak of the Second World War in 1939, it often seems to be the month when Things Happen. This is reflected in the publishing world, too: many of the 'important' books of the year start appearing on the shelves of bookshops.

It is a time to take a deep breath and reset a little bit, turning our attention to the kinds of books we read at school when we were 15. You may be pleasantly surprised to find they are not nearly as boring as you remember. Perhaps we could even sneak some non-fiction in for a real change of pace. Equipped with the right reading material, you will be ready to pack up your rucksack with freshly sharpened pencils and a brand new notebook, excited for what awaits you between the pages.

BILBO'S BIRTHDAY

'When Mr Bilbo Baggins of Bag End announced that he would shortly be celebrating his eleventy-first birthday with a party of special magnificence, there was much talk and excitement in Hobbiton...' Thus begins the Lord of the Rings trilogy. Bilbo Baggins happens to share his birthday with another hobbit named Frodo: 22 September. On the big day itself, *'The sun got up, the clouds vanished, flags were unfurled and the fun began.'* There is music and games, food and drink, but the climax is a firework display organized by the wizard Gandalf culminating in a very lifelike dragon that scares everyone to bits, until Bilbo merrily declares that it is just the signal for supper – or so he claims...

Things Fall Apart

BY CHINUA ACHEBE (1958)

'He grew rapidly like a yam tendril in the rainy season.' Similes like this are a repeated reminder that *Things Fall Apart*, about tribal life in Nigeria towards the end of the 19th century, is an entirely different literary experience to many of the other curriculum classics taught in school. How I wish this had been one of my set texts rather than *The Duchess of Malfi* (yawn) and *Jane Eyre* (fine, but, you know). If this book is sitting on your shelf right now, go grab it immediately – you have been missing out.

Chinua Achebe was born in Nigeria in 1930. After graduating from the University of Ibadan, he went to work as a radio producer for the Nigerian Broadcasting Corporation, while also managing to find the time to write. *Things Fall Apart* was his first novel, published when he was 28. When civil war broke out in 1967 when the south-eastern region of Biafra sought to break away from the rest of Nigeria, Achebe became a vocal supporter of independence, frequently appealing to foreign observers for support and aid. Frustrated by the lack of progress, he took up various teaching positions in the United States in the 1970s, settling there for good in the 1990s.

The story of how *Things Fall Apart* found a publisher is one to strike fear into the heart of authors everywhere. Achebe sent the handwritten manuscript – the only copy in the world – to an agency in London to have it typed up, but they misplaced it. Can you imagine?! It was not until his boss happened to be going to England that she was able to track it down to a dusty corner of the agency's office.

Achebe then sent it to a publisher, who in turn passed it on to a professor at the London School of Economics who had recently returned from Africa, in the hope that he would be able to offer an opinion on this (at the time) unusual text. According to Achebe, 'He wrote what they said was the shortest report they ever had on any novel – seven words: "The best first novel since the war".'

Things Fall Apart is about, well, how things fall apart. The title comes from a W B Yeats poem called 'The Second Coming' (1919): 'Things fall apart; the centre cannot hold; / Mere anarchy is loosed upon the world.' The story traces the fate of Okonkwo, a chieftan in the Igbo tribe with three wives, eight children, and five human heads hanging on the wall of his hut in honour of his bravery in battle. Many of my favourite passages are about food: the yam foo-foo and bitter leaf soup they eat for supper, the basket of plantains and coco-yams and a small pot of palm oil that Okonkwo's youngest wife brings round to a friend's house as a gift, the egusi soup and pots of palm-wine that's served up at a feast. It is a colourful and detailed portrayal of rural life in Nigeria before colonization.

But then the British arrive, bashing people up with Bibles rather than guns, but the effect is similar: utter devastation. There are concerns that the 'white man had indeed brought a lunatic religion, but he had also built a trading store...' Conflict ensues, resulting in a narrative that has much in common with literature from other cultures addressing parallel themes, for example New Zealand writer Patricia Grace's excellent novel *Potiki* (1986) about a Maori community that is threatened with destruction.

The language in *Things Fall Apart* has a different rhythm to that in much of the Anglo–American literary canon and is all the more interesting for it. In a 1965 essay entitled 'The African Writer and the English Language', Achebe explained that conveying the African experience required 'a new English, still in full communion with its ancestral home but altered to suit its new African surroundings.' Achebe's writing style is deceptively simple and he is a genius at understatement; this is not a book to be read casually or with only one eye (as it were).

Things Fall Apart was the first 'hit' novel written in the English language that portrayed Africa from an African point of view, rather than a colonial one. Achebe, of course, had literary predecessors, in particular Amos Tutuola with *The Palm-Wine Drinkard* (1952) and Cyprian Ekwensi with *People of the City* (1954), but they did not achieve the mainstream success that he did. It provided a welcome stylistic contrast to the likes of John Buchan, Joyce Cary and Joseph Conrad (whose books manage to be both racist and boring, a doubly terrible crime). Ultimately *Things Fall Apart* is about how horrifying it is to the mind, the body and the soul when unwanted, uninvited change is imposed upon us. Never did a back-to-school text seem so pertinent or so profound.

The Fortnight in September

BY R C SHERRIFF (1931)

This quiet, unassuming novel about a family of four on their annual seaside holiday is about nothing and yet, at the same time, about everything – as the author R C Sherriff put it in his autobiography, the 'drama of the undramatic'. The book is a slow unfolding, as Sherriff explains, 'a day-by-day account of [a family's] holiday, from their last evening at home until the day they packed their bags for their return; how they came out of their shabby boarding house every morning and went down to the sea.' If the plot of *The Fortnight in September* was pitched to a Hollywood producer, it would instantly be rejected because there is no conflict. Although the suspense is modest (the stress of crossing platforms at Clapham Junction station, a worrying moment when it seems that the family will not be able to rent a beach hut), these perfectly described scenes are vivid and meaningful, and the quality of writing makes the novel soar.

Sherriff uses everyday language to describe his everyday people, never patronizing but allowing the reader to see the complicated feelings that all the characters carry with them, yet do not share with each other. Everyone has their backstory, which is gradually revealed, and I felt pangs of empathy and recognition with each of them in turn.

The head of the family, Mr Stevens, is a little pompous, writing out 'Marching Orders' and 'impressively' bringing his wife a cup of tea in bed (so unprecedented it makes her tearful). But his careful and thoughtful planning means that everything goes as it should. He loves arranging things but 'he knew that it had to be done very carefully, and never pressed his plans against general opposition.' Every other day is left 'absolutely free for everyone to do what they liked', which 'added tremendously to the pleasure of mealtimes, because each returned with different experiences to describe', an approach that many of us could learn from.

Mrs Stevens teeters on the verge of pathetic, with her travel anxiety, longing for comfortable shoes and inability to admit her real feelings. But she is a loyal if inarticulate wife as well as a very attentive mother to the children, who are lively, thoughtful, mostly kind to their mother, yet each living their own lives quite separately from the family. Mary, the daughter, has a holiday romance that could have been casually written off by Sherriff as trivial or even sordid. But he describes her adventure so vividly: her touching naivety, the 'frightening feeling of unreality' when she is alone in a crowd, wondering if she will recognize her new friend, and trying to calm herself: 'It's Bognor! Dear old Bognor – don't worry – you know Bognor!'

The Fortnight in September is a superb reminder that the simple life may be the key to happiness: the importance of family, the pleasure to be found in daily rituals, and paying close attention to the world around us. When Mary goes to visit their next-door neighbour, she experiences the strange dislocation of being in a house that is somehow exactly the same but different. 'There was a rack, just like theirs, in Mrs Haykin's hall – but how different it looked! A solitary, curious little bonnet hung from one peg and a grey woollen scarf from another, but the rest were empty. Mary could never remember seeing an empty peg in their own hall at home: if you took a coat off there was always something underneath.' There is always something underneath, Sherriff seems to be saying, if we take the time to look below the surface and find the (sometimes unexpected) depths of meaning.

Top ten school curriculum classics
that are not nearly as boring as you remember them

1/War and Peace
by Leo Tolstoy (1869)

2/Orlando
by Virginia Woolf (1928)

3/Great Expectations
by Charles Dickens (1861)

4/The Color Purple
by Alice Walker (1982)

5/Native Son
by Richard Wright (1940)

6/A Passage to India
by E M Forster (1924)

7/Tess of the D'Urbervilles
by Thomas Hardy (1891)

8/Beloved
by Toni Morrison (1987)

9/Vanity Fair
by William Thackeray (1848)

10/Of Mice and Men
by John Steinbeck (1937)

Zora Neale Hurston
Queen of the Harlem Renaissance

A curriculum classic that deserves immediate revisiting is Zora Neale Hurston's *Their Eyes Were Watching God* (1937). Born in Alabama and growing up in Florida, Hurston began her career as an anthropologist, with African–American traditions her primary area of research. She published a number of non-fiction essays on the subject, as well as some short stories, but it was *Their Eyes Were Watching God*, her second novel, which turned out to be her most enduring piece of writing. Penned in the immediate aftermath of an unhappy love affair, mostly while conducting field work in Haiti, it follows the intense, moving story of Janie Crawford's three attempts at marriage in early 20th-century Florida. She at last finds love with a younger man named Tea Cake, but tragedy ensues.

Focus on...

A classic text of the Harlem Renaissance, *Their Eyes Were Watching God* was not an immediate success, but finally achieved recognition a couple of decades after Hurston's death as readers learnt to marvel at the stylistic originality of this magnificent tale of one woman coming to consciousness for the very first time.

A novel set amid the rhythms of the academic year

Normal People by Sally Rooney (2018)

I hated this book the first time I read it. I did not see the point of it at all. But perhaps a little bit like falling in love, it took perseverance and patience – and watching the TV adaptation – and then, finally, I was able to see it clearly for what it was. Set during on-off couple Marianne and Connell's last years at school and first years at university, it is a bold, brave evocation of first love. Its simple, direct dialogue tricks you into thinking it is quite a straightforward book, but eventually I 'got' how insightful it is in its own quiet way about how difficult it can be to communicate with the one we love, how hideous and painful the whole experience can be, and yet how life-changing: 'He brought her goodness like a gift and now it belongs to her. Meanwhile his life opens out before him in all directions at once. They've done a lot of good for each other.' In the end, for me, it was a beautiful reading experience: awkward, frustrating, tender.

A glimpse of the world from another angle – even another planet...

The Midwich Cuckoos by John Wyndham (1957)

This book opens on 26 September and the initial tone and setting are misleadingly low-key: everyday life in a small English village where nothing much happens and everyone knows each other – except then, overnight, all the women of child-bearing age, both the married and (gasp!) the unmarried, suddenly find themselves pregnant by aliens and, well, you can imagine the kerfuffle. In precise prose, philosophical at times, Wyndham explores society's response to the idea of difference in such a fascinating way. It's zippy and lively and feels incredibly realistic about what happens when catastrophe strikes.

Top 20 non-fiction books – *because*
September demands a change of pace

1/*The Warmth of Other Suns*
by Isabel Wilkerson (2010)
This re-telling of the mass migration of African Americans out of the American South is genuinely revelatory, utterly gripping and impossible to forget.

2/*Barbarian Days: A Surfing Life*
by William Finnegan (2015)
Even if you have no interest in surfing, this terrific memoir about the sea and the soul and everything in between is incredibly insightful and moving about male identity.

3/*Far From The Tree: Parents, Children and the Search for Identity* by Andrew Solomon (2012)
The best book I have ever read on parenting – and it's not even really about parenting.

4/*Shapely Ankle Preferr'd: A History of the Lonely Hearts Ad*
by Francesca Beauman (2011)
Cannot think why I included this one…

5/*A Pattern Language: Towns, Buildings, Construction*
by Christopher Alexander (1977)
The interiors book that influenced all other interiors books, even if they don't know it. After reading it, having a sofa in your kitchen will become your primary goal in life.

6/*Factory Girls: Voices from the Heart of Modern China*
by Leslie T Chang (2008)
Utterly fascinating about working-class women's lives in modern China. Beautifully written, too. A quiet gem.

7/*Between the World and Me*
by Ta-Nehisi Coates (2015)
This collection of essays about how it feels to be a black man in modern America, written by one of the greatest public intellectuals of our age, is highly original and eye-opening.

8/*The Invisible Woman: The Story of Nelly Ternan and Charles Dickens* by Claire Tomalin (1990)
Tomalin is pretty much my favourite non-fiction writer and I will always devour her every word. Not to be confused with…

9/*Invisible Women: Exposing Data Bias in a World Designed for Men*
by Caroline Criado Perez (2019)
It is no exaggeration to say that this book will genuinely change the way you move through the world. You will also never look at iPhones, piano keyboards or the driver's seat in a car the same way again.

10/*Vivien: The Life of Vivien Leigh*
by Alexander Walker (1987)

I am a sucker for a biography of an Old Hollywood star: around the age of 14 and 15, they were all I read. This is one of the best: gossipy but empathetic, as well as stuffed full of diamonds.

11/The Unwomanly Face of War: An Oral History of Women in World War II
by Svetlana Alexievich (1985)
A clever and moving re-telling of the story of the Second World War from an entirely different and under-appreciated angle.

12/Becoming Beyoncé: The Untold Story by J Randy Taraborrelli (2015)
Just trust me, OK?

13/Do No Harm: Stories of Life, Death and Brain Surgery
by Henry Marsh (2014)
A brain surgeon writes about his experiences drilling into people's heads. Mind-blowing (pun intended).

14/Georgiana, Duchess of Devonshire
by Amanda Foreman (1998)
In many ways the original O G when it comes to popular, accessible, social history.

15/Ghost of the Tsunami: Death and Life in Japan's Disaster Zone
by Richard Lloyd Parry (2017)
Offers a greater insight into Japanese life and culture than any number of more conventional takes. Highly readable, hugely enriching.

16/Them: A Memoir of Parents
by Francine du Plessix Gray (2005)
A gorgeous evocation of family, New York and publishing – I mean, what else is there?

17/A People's Tragedy: The Russian Revolution, 1891–1924
by Orlando Figes (1996)
A classic history book of the finest order: impeccable research, genuine insight and easy to read.

18/How To Fail: Everything I've Ever Learned from Things Going Wrong by Elizabeth Day (2019)
The only self-help book worth reading. A profoundly compassionate, highly entertaining guide to life.

19/Nora: A Biography of Nora Joyce by Brenda Maddox (1988)
A beautifully written biography of Nora Barnacle, who married James Joyce. Riveting about love, lust, marriage; to what extent did she influence Joyce's art? (Answer: more than a lot).

20/A Swim in the Pond in the Rain: In Which Four Russians Give a Masterclass on Writing, Reading, and Life
by George Saunders (2021)
Saunders talks the reader through some Russian short stories in his characteristically warm, kind, erudite way – it's a treat to spend time in his company.

January
February
March
April
May
June
July
August
September

October

November
December

Listen! The wind is rising, and the air is wild with leaves,
We have had our summer evenings, now for October eves!

Humbert Wolfe, 'Autumn (Resignation)' (1926)

W hile the leaves turning red and falling from the trees is one of the most pervasive clichés to exist in literature, in actuality it is often the quality of the light that really makes October so spectacularly special: a kind of misty, golden light that coats everything with a sense of mysteriousness. Suddenly matters of the supernatural no longer seem quite so far-fetched. So, as autumn unashamedly announces its arrival, let's be sure to hunker down with a book that matches this mood.

October is, in many respects, defined by Halloween, named for All Hallow's Eve, which is the night before All Hallows, a feast day that traditionally honoured any Christian who had died and gone to heaven. In the 21st century, however, Halloween has more to do with fire-unsafe polyester costumes and alarmingly fluorescent sweets. Trick-or-treating, that most ubiquitous of Halloween activities, also has roots in Christian tradition – specifically a custom known as 'souling', whereby people travelled from parish to parish begging the rich for cake in exchange for praying for their souls.

Typically, therefore, a book lover might turn to the scariest of offerings at this time of year. In the past, this might have meant picking up the likes of *Frankenstein* by Mary Shelley (1818) (surprisingly dull: Shelley spends the first half droning on in a vague way about science and philosophy and the story takes an age to get going) or *Dracula* by Bram Stoker (1897) (surprisingly excellent: Stoker offers a magnificently twisty-turny plot that keeps you engaged in the characters at every turn).

I am confident, however, that we can improve on these two 19th-century classics that between them did so much to define the horror genre. The aim is for the pile of books on our bedside table this month to be just like a trick-or-treat basket: some sweet and some bitter, some newfangled and some old school, some hard and some soft – each one a delight in a different way.

DELICIOUS AUTUMN

Is not this a true autumn day? Just the still melancholy that I love – that makes life and nature harmonise. The birds are consulting about their migrations, the trees are putting on the hectic or the pallid hues of decay, and begin to strew the ground, that one's very footsteps may not disturb the repose of earth and air, while they give us a scent that is a perfect anodyne to the restless spirit. Delicious autumn! My very soul is wedded to it, and if I were a bird, I would fly about the earth seeking the successive autumns.

Letter from George Eliot to Maria Lewis,
1 October 1841

The Moonstone

BY WILKIE COLLINS (1868)

Wilkie Collins is (almost) the only writer that my husband and I both admire equally (yes, we have very different taste in literature: there is no tale of a gruesome murder in 13th-century Constantinople that that man will not devour...), which is in part why we named one of our children Wilkie in his honour. It remains an unusual name and we rarely come across others who share it, with the exception of Wilkie Twycross in the *Harry Potter* books (the apparition instructor from the Ministry of Magic).

Wilkie Collins was born in London in 1824, the son of a landscape painter. From an early age he suffered from a number of life-limiting ailments, hobbling and coughing his way around London, often in a haze of laudanum, fearing himself pursued by a green-skinned woman with tusks (don't we all?). Famously he never married, instead maintaining two families that he seemed to enjoy and love equally: his companion Caroline Graves (whom he is thought to have met when they got chatting in the street in the Tottenham Court Road area of London near where they both lived) and the mother of his children Martha Rudd (she was working in a pub in Winterton-on-Sea near where he researched *The Moonstone*).

The Moonstone is a romp of a tale, set mostly in a country house in Yorkshire. On her 18th birthday, Rachel Verinder inherits a diamond from her uncle, who is an officer in the British army in India; she wears it to her birthday party and that night it is stolen from her bedroom – but by whom? Written almost entirely while Collins was high on laudanum and based in part on stories about goings-on in India that he heard while at his gentlemen's club, the Athenaeum, it is a riotous adventure that includes everything from snake worship to Indian jugglers to unsolved murders to passionate love affairs, as well as all sorts of other thrills along the way.

Let us note at this point, however, that Collins is famously terrible at endings, and *The Moonstone* is no exception (no spoilers, don't worry). But with a plot this busy, no wonder he was exhausted by the time he wrote the last line:

> *So the years pass, and repeat each other; so the same events revolve in the cycles of time. What will be the next adventure of the Moonstone? Who can tell!*

I immediately warmed to *The Moonstone* for the way it champions the oppressed: women, servants, indigenous people, those with disabilities. Collins makes a number of small but radical gestures to this end in both plot and character – for example, in his portrayal of sexual desire in housemaid Rosanna Spearman, who is a woman with disabilities. In this way he encourages the reader to think about what role Rosanna might play in the Victorian heterosexual economy; could it be that her situation liberates her from conventional expectations, opening more doors (rather than fewer) with regards to how she lives her life? It was (and, up to a point, still is) rare to place a woman with disabilities at the centre of a romantic narrative and hence it is invigorating to watch Collins do so in his own inimitable way.

The Moonstone is widely considered to be the first detective novel ever written. Naturally, there had been writers before who had incorporated some elements of a detective story (Edgar Allen Poe in his short stories or Charles Dickens in *Bleak House*), but Collins made it his everything. He incorporated a number of now-familiar

tropes: the gentleman detective pitted against the bungling local policeman, an English country house setting, plenty of red herrings followed by a final dramatic plot twist, and so on. As a result, *The Moonstone* has, over the years, been the inspiration for a number of classic detective novels by such writers as Sir Arthur Conan Doyle and Agatha Christie, and more recently by the likes of Sarah Waters with *Fingersmith* (2002) or Sara Collins with *The Confessions of Frannie Langton* (2019).

The 1860s was an extraordinarily prolific period for Collins. *The Moonstone* was his fourth novel in a row to be a bestseller, coming directly after *The Woman in White* (1860), *No Name* (1862), and *Armadale* (1866). As his publisher later recalled:

During the run of The Moonstone *as a serial there were scenes in Wellington Street [in Covent Garden] that doubtless did the author's and publisher's hearts good. And especially when the serial was nearing its ending, on publishing days there would be quite a crowd of anxious readers waiting for the new number, and I know of several bets that were made as to where the moonstone would be found at last. Even the porters and boys were interested in the story, and read the new number in sly corners, and often with their packs on their backs...*

It is no wonder. High on suspense (because it was written as a serial, it is full of cliffhangers), not as po-faced as Dickens (gasp, but it is true), and featuring vocabulary on every page that reads like the most delicious parody of a 19th-century blockbuster and yet it is the real deal, *The Moonstone* is a Fun-with-a-capital-F literary experience. You will turn the last page with a similar feeling to that of having eaten your entire haul of Halloween sweets all in one go: overstimulated, overtired, overjoyed.

Harriet

BY ELIZABETH JENKINS (1934)

*H*arriet is a deeply upsetting novel, which perhaps does not sound like a great recommendation, and indeed it is not for the faint-hearted. Based on the true story of Harriet Staunton who was subjected to the most horrific neglect by her husband, it was written and published 32 years before *In Cold Blood* by Truman Capote (1966); the difference was that, unlike Capote, Elizabeth Jenkins did not proudly proclaim that she had invented an entirely new genre, 'true crime'. Quite the opposite: within a decade of its publication, after news of Nazi concentration camps was broadcast to an appalled world, igniting a debate about how ordinary people came to be persuaded to perform acts of the utmost evil, Jenkins even went as far as to disown *Harriet* – because, as she put it, 'the horror of the story weighed on my mind and became more acutely painful as time went on.'

Harriet begins with a superb evocation of suburban life in 1870s London, all the details gorgeously and imaginatively described. Harriet herself is a young woman with learning differences (a 'natural', as the Victorians would have called her) who is cherished by her mother, has inherited money, and has a perfectly happy life. But then she meets Lewis and is seduced into marriage; she is 34 and he is 24. Her distraught mother is told by the doctor, 'you must see that what she's doing now is done by hundreds of young women...alarming her friends by wanting to throw herself away on a worthless young man.' Lewis forbids Harriet to see her mother and from there it only gets

worse: she is deprived of food, denied a doctor's attentions, and forced to stay in her bedroom in what today would be understood as a classic case of coercive control.

The book is written with admirable discretion and subtlety, and although the reader does watch in horror (and incredulity) as Harriet heads towards her terrible fate, the book is not salacious or distasteful. Its impact comes afterwards when you have finished it and you sit and think about the implications of what you have just read.

The running question throughout is whether Lewis and his accomplices (three family members and the girl he later marries) intended to do what they did. In real life, when the case came to trial (it was known as the Penge Mystery), it was never determined how guilty they really were – guilty of not looking after Harriet, not feeding her properly, certainly; but guilty of plotting to murder her, who knows?

This is an absorbing and ingenious novel, in large part due to the way Jenkins evokes Victorian comfort and domesticity, but then subverts it by introducing a creeping sense of horror. Her achievement is all the more powerful when you realize that she based Harriet on a non-fiction book called *The Trial of the Stauntons* (1911), which reprints the actual court transcript; but it was solely her own imagination that allowed her to suggest how such evil could be carried out with such commonplace ease, in fact 'with almost unbelievable callousness and cruelty' as she wrote in her memoir when she was in her 90s.

Elizabeth Jenkins was born in 1905, the daughter of a headmaster, and over the course of her career wrote both fiction and non-fiction, making her unusually well placed to produce this hybrid piece. While *The Tortoise and the Hare* (1954) may be her most famous novel, in my view *Harriet* is by far the more interesting one. You will not be able to get the deeply memorable plot out of your head for ages afterwards: it offers a truly terrifying reminder that we all have it in us to turn to the dark side.

Daphne du Maurier
Queen of the psychological thriller

Who better to read in October than Daphne du Maurier? Born in London in 1907 into a family who loved literature, theatre and art, du Maurier's first novel, *The Loving Spirit* (1931), which takes its title from an Emily Brontë poem, came out when she was 24. Half a decade later she had a bestseller on her hands with *Jamaica Inn* (1936), a highly entertaining story about smuggling set on the Cornish moors. She soon married and shipped out to Egypt, where her new husband had been posted by the British army; she hated it there and out of her misery emerged *Rebecca* (1938), also a bestseller. 'It's a bit on the gloomy side,' she told her publisher when she delivered the manuscript, and she wasn't wrong. It is a brilliant, original, chilling book. Du Maurier settled in Cornwall with her three children during the Second World War, and continued to write; her output included a number of enduring short stories such as *The Birds* (1952), *Don't Look Now* (1971), *The Doll* (published posthumously in 2011) and one of my favourite novels of hers, *The Scapegoat* (1957). This last is about a university lecturer who meets his doppelganger while on holiday in France and ends up entangled. Her novels rarely have a happy ending, actually.

Focus on...

Two novels about lost souls

Lincoln in the Bardo by George Saunders (2017)

Saunders vividly re-imagines Abraham Lincoln's visits to the cemetery in which his son is buried following his sudden death from typhoid fever at the age of 11. The cemetery turns out to be inhabited by spirits who refuse to accept the fact that they are dead and hence exist in the 'bardo', a rather lovely Tibetan word meaning the 'state between life and death'. The spirits constitute the main narrative voice throughout, which I know makes it sounds as if this is going to be a weird, difficult book, but conversely it is a genuinely accessible and entertaining one. I found it really beautiful.

An American Marriage by Tayari Jones (2018)

I adored Jones's novel about the impact of a wrongful arrest on an African–American couple living in Atlanta named Celestial and Roy, and I am certain you will, too. A dark, sad vision of America in which richly drawn characters live out many people's worst nightmare. The book is incredibly moving about a thwarted love, utterly gripping, and yet desperately sad. It is impossible not to sob and sob at the end – drying one's tears only to go and seek out the rest of Jones's back catalogue, starting with *Silver Sparrow* (2011).

Top ten dark and chilly novels

1/*Mexican Gothic*
by Silvia Moreno-Garcia (2020)
A re-imagining of Gothic fantasy set in the Mexican countryside in the 1950s, in which a young woman investigates claims made in a frantic letter from her cousin that her new husband is trying to kill her. A gripping period thriller.

2/*The Mysteries of Udolpho*
by Ann Radcliffe (1794)
This tale of a young French woman who is orphaned and imprisoned in a castle in Italy is generally considered one of the very first Gothic novels. Elements of the supernatural combine with a highly melodramatic romance to create a reading experience of the most splendidly sensational kind.

3/*Elizabeth Is Missing*
by Emma Healey (2014)
An elderly woman with dementia tries to work out why her friend has disappeared. An affecting, compelling detective story that also gets to grips with the terrible impact of cognitive decline.

4/*Drive Your Plow Over the Bones of the Dead*
by Olga Tokarczuk (2009)
A murder mystery by this Nobel Prize winning Polish author about an unconventional woman in her sixties whose dogs go missing in the middle of winter, from the tiny village on the Polish/Czech border where she lives. A whodunit of the weirdest and most wonderful kind.

5/*The Girl with the Dragon Tattoo*
by Stieg Larsson (2005)
A Swedish crime thriller starring computer hacker Lisbeth Salander about corruption and murder in the corporate world. A bit gory in parts for my taste, but maybe you like that sort of thing.

6/*White is for Witching*
by Helen Oyeyemi (2009)
A terrifying novel about a haunted house in Dover on the south coast of England – to say more would be to give away the secrets of this unconventional and accomplished piece of writing.

7/Gone Girl

by Gillian Flynn (2012)
Such a page-turner that by the time you have finished you will be covered in sweat having not showered for three days, it will be dark outside, and your dog/children/partner will be crying for food and attention. Emotionally manipulative but all the more entertaining for it – you are being taken for a ride, but you know it and love it. The suspense is off the scale.

8/Hagar's Daughter

by Pauline Hopkins (1901)
Thought to be the first detective story by an African–American woman, this novel is more of a historical artefact than anything else, but that has value in itself. A young black maid wears men's clothing to try to solve a series of mysteries, getting involved along the way with a kidnapping plot, mistaken identity and murder.

9/The Long Drop

by Denise Mina (2017)
The best kind of crime fiction. Set in Glasgow in the 1950s and based on the story of one of the last men in Scotland to be hanged, the serial killer Peter Manuel, this is an extraordinary feat of imagination; gruesome, but without being overly salacious.

10/Devil's Day

by Andrew Michael Hurley (2017)
'What is a ghost, after all, but the past enduring in a strange and incomprehensible form?' Indeed. This tale of Gothic ritual and horror set in the Lancashire uplands – a part of the world that has been largely missed off the map in terms of literary fiction, even though it is so rich in stories – is an extraordinary, beautiful, creepy book.

January
February
March
April
May
June
July
August
September
October
November
December

'November is the most disagreeable month in the whole year,' said Margaret, standing at the window one dull afternoon, looking out at the frostbitten garden.

'That's the reason I was born in it,' observed Jo pensively, quite unconscious of the blot on her nose.

Louisa May Alcott, *Little Women* (1868)

F Scott Fitzgerald once described November as 'crisp and energetic', but I am not sure I entirely agree. Certainly there is a change in the air as winter wraps its cloak ever more tightly around us. In the northern hemisphere, the cold weather encourages plants to hide away in anticipation of the gaudy display of spring; meanwhile many animal species tend to behave in a similar fashion, fattening themselves up in readiness for a long winter's sleep. In the southern hemisphere, summer is on the horizon.

November is a month in which we honour the dead. In early November comes the Day of the Dead, also known as *Día de los Muertos*, a Mexican holiday associated with the Catholic celebration All Saints' Day. This often has an air of magic realism to it, so it seems appropriate that this month's reading list reflects this, potentially offering some mental respite from what can be a rather bleak month.

November also honours Armistice Day, a commemoration of the First World War ceasefire, which took place at 11am on the 11th day of the 11th month in 1918. One way to remember the sacrifice made by so many is to immerse ourselves in novels that help us understand and empathize with the experiences of combatants on all sides.

Let us agree, then, that November is a time of sober contemplation. There is a yearning to seek out books that are brooding, melancholy and have a miserable ending but, equally, that make you feel like you have somehow moved forward – that things are going to get better, just wait and see.

LEAVES ALONG THE WIND

The world is tired, the year is old,
The little leaves are glad to die,
The wind goes shivering with cold
Among the rushes dry.

Our love is dying like the grass,
And we who kissed grow coldly kind,
Half glad to see our poor love pass
Like leaves along the wind.

Sara Teasdale,
'November' (1911)

The Bluest Eye

BY TONI MORRISON (1970)

The first African–American woman to win the Nobel Prize in Literature, Toni Morrison was the author of 11 novels. Her superpower was to place a young black girl at the centre of all her stories, while also managing to sustain ongoing critical and commercial success. Her oeuvre is unblinkingly sad, disruptive and disquieting, but at the same time features moments of dazzling lyrical beauty and encourages quiet reflection a-plenty; it thus suits one's mood in November just perfectly.

Toni Morrison was born Chloe Wofford in 1931. Aged 12 she was baptized a Catholic and took the name of Anthony after Anthony of Padua, which she later shortened to Toni; meanwhile Morrison was acquired from her first, brief husband. She attended Howard University followed by Cornell, where she wrote a thesis titled 'Virginia Woolf's and William Faulkner's Treatment of the Alienated', later returning to Howard to teach while also raising two small children and getting up at 4am every day to write. Her first novel, *The Bluest Eye*, published when she was 39, was the result, and it is an excellent introduction to all that makes Morrison's writing so spectacular.

The Bluest Eye is about 11-year-old Pecola Breedlove from small-town Ohio (the same town, in fact, where Morrison herself grew up). The narrative is divided into four seasons, beginning with autumn:

Quiet as it's kept, there were no marigolds in the fall of 1941.

We thought, at the time, that it was because Pecola was having her father's baby that the marigolds did not grow...

Morrison's genius shines through in this powerful opening line, dispensing with narrative suspense and instead exhorting the reader to stick around to find out not what happened, but why it happened. 'What was driving me to write was the silence – so many stories untold and unexamined,' she later commented.

Morrison was inspired to write *The Bluest Eye* by a conversation she had as a child in which a friend had argued there could not be a God because her prayers for blue eyes had not been answered. The terrible impact that white beauty standards in the media and elsewhere can have on a young black girl's sense of identity is central to the novel: the doomed Pecola desperately wants to resemble her heroine, Shirley Temple, the archetypal blue-eyed, blonde-haired star. Morrison asks the reader to think about how racial self-loathing is learned – and, perhaps more importantly, how it can be un-learned.

I am also fascinated by Morrison's analysis of what she calls 'funk'. She writes about how, at an early age, a certain sort of 'thin brown girl' is taught the 'careful development of thrift, patience, high morals and good manners. In short, how to get rid of the funkiness. The dreadful funkiness of passion, the funkiness of nature, the funkiness of the wide range of human emotions.'

To me, this passage powerfully recalls a more recent piece of writing about the inner lives of women by Elena Ferrante. What Morrison calls 'funk', Ferrante calls '*frantumaglia*'. It is a theme to which Morrison returns in her second novel, *Sula* (1973), which – though it is set in an African–American neighbourhood in Ohio in the 1900s – has much in common with (and perhaps even formed the inspiration for) Ferrante's Neapolitan quartet in its striking depiction of an intense relationship between two childhood friends.

The Bluest Eye is written in a mostly straightforward tone, interspersed with flashes of poetry of the fiercest beauty. Morrison spoke about how 'street language is lyrical, plus it has this blend of the standard English and the sermonic, as well as the colloquial, you know – that is what I wanted to polish and show, and make it a literary vehicle.' She undoubtedly succeeded, incorporating oral traditions as well as elements of magic realism, which cumulatively serve to underscore the harrowing nature of the various personal tragedies that her characters are forced to endure.

The Bluest Eye is thus the first step in a journey that within 17 years, with the publication of Morrison's most celebrated novel, *Beloved* (1987), would win her a Pulitzer Prize in honour of her unique, brave talent for exploring black identity in America.

The Road

BY CORMAC MCCARTHY (2006)

Gosh, how I sobbed when I finished this book! I implore you to attempt it only if you are feeling sufficiently emotionally robust. It starts gently: 'When he woke in the woods in the dark and the cold of the night he'd reach out to touch the child sleeping beside him.' But then we are told: 'Nights dark beyond darkness and the days more grey each one than what had gone before. Like the onset of some cold glaucoma dimming away the world.'

The protagonist, known only as 'the man', is walking south with his son to escape the cold of the oncoming winter. We understand fairly quickly that some sort of catastrophe has overtaken Earth, although we are not sure what and when; cold grey ash is covering everything. 'By day the banished sun circles the Earth like a grieving mother with a lamp.' But it is worse than this because the catastrophe has unleashed not only many, many refugees, but a horrible spate of killing and mutilation. The road is dangerous as well as arduous.

Against the background of this unnameable catastrophe, the writing is all too precise, capturing the reader in a hypnotic grip:

The man watched him. Real life is pretty bad?
What do you think?
Well, I think we're still here. A lot of bad things have happened but we're still here.
Yeah.

You don't think that's so great.
It's okay.

Its directness. Its bleakness. Its lack of punctuation! I found it completely unlike anything I had read before, leading me not-so-gently by the hand towards a new and startling form of language. Stylistically it recalls Hemingway in some ways, but with a modern spin that is even more uncompromising, offering the reader no social niceties, refusing to make life easy. You know how sometimes a lot of novels feel the same? Like you have read them before but maybe just forgot? *The Road* most certainly does not.

At the centre of the story is the man's love for his son. Within the horror of the journey, he tries to make it bearable for the anxious boy, and they have occasional, slightly reassuring dialogues. Glimmers of hope are offered to the reader such as when the man and his son find an abandoned house in which to sleep and scavenge for food. But for the man 'the boy was all that stood between him and death'. Food is important, when they can find it: mushrooms or a can of beans. So is the man's pistol, protecting them against other travellers they come across 'shuffling through the ash casting their hooded heads from side to side. Some of them wearing canister masks, one in a biohazard suit.' There are scenes where they directly encounter the occasional fellow refugee, who may or may not be a threat – even the reader is not sure.

The Road's power lies in its plausibility. The tender relationship between the man and his son gives the reader some human relief, but also forces one to identify with the awful, extended ordeal that they experience together. In *The Road* McCarthy, who was born in 1933, grew up in Tennessee and now lives in Santa Fe, has created a 21st-century mythic journey: if you can cope with it, you will never forget it.

For many years, I assumed this novel was not for me: too bleak, too dystopian, maybe even too 'male' (whatever that means). But I surprised myself and found it utterly emotionally shattering in the most exhilarating way. I dare you to read this, even and especially if it seems outside your comfort zone. You will find within its pages a miserable but redemptive journey – rather like the thirty days of November, in fact.

A few more tales of a life-changing journey

The Salmon Who Dared to Leap Higher by Ahn Do-hyon (2015)

The Grapes of Wrath by John Steinbeck (1939)

The Hundred-Year-Old Man Who Climbed Out of the Window and Disappeared by Jonas Jonasson (2012)

The Far Cry by Emma Smith (1949)

The End We Start From by Megan Hunter (2017)

Miss Austen by Gill Hornby (2020)

Flights by Olga Tokarczuk (2017)

A Countess Below Stairs by Eva Ibbotson (1981)

The Fishermen by Chigozie Obioma (2015)

Margaret Atwood
Inventor of other worlds

In a month where we are seeking the slightly surreal and melancholy in our reading, Canadian writer Margaret Atwood offers an embarrassment of riches. From the unnervingly believable dystopian future of *The Handmaid's Tale* (1985) to the fictional account of a real-life Canadian murderess in *Alias Grace* (1996) and *Hag-Seed* (2016), a reworking of William Shakespeare's *The Tempest*, Atwood is so prolific and genre-defying that you could probably find something within her canon to suit each month of the year. Since 1961 she has written 17 novels, 10 non-fiction books, 8 short stories and 8 children's books, as well as graphic novels, poetry, and scripts for TV and radio. Phew! Not a list to dwell on when one is feeling unproductive.

Focus on...

Growing up in rural northern Canada, Atwood's childhood home had no TV, movies or radio available, no theatre and no libraries, but plenty of books. Comic strips were her first reading material and these, along with a book on the solar system and 'a dollop of Greek mythology', fed the first imaginative worlds she created.

Atwood has written that 'like a great many children before me and since, I was an inventor of other worlds'. And this is what her fiction does so wonderfully. Whether the dystopian future conjured up in *Oryx and Crake* (2003), twentieth-century Canada of *The Blind Assassin* (2001), or the Greek underworld of *The Penelopiad* (2005), each novel transports you to somewhere completely different and you will emerge, slightly discombobulated, with a fresh perspective on the world, and hungry for more.

Two books about different aspects of November

One Hundred Years of Solitude
by Gabriel García Márquez (1967)

Born in Colombia in 1928, Márquez started out as a journalist, but ended up inventing an entirely new literary genre that is just what is called for during the month of November: magic realism. This delicious novel opens with a family tree, but don't let that put you off. It is the story of several generations of the Buendía family that will also make you want to visit South America immediately. It is a chaotic saga of family and fantasy that interweaves the real and the fantastical like a dazzling dream. This book changed me a little, opening my eyes to what literature can do. Hopefully it will do the same for you.

Also Try

All Quiet on the Western Front
by Erich Maria Remarque (1929)

To be read in honour of the end of the First World War. Its title in the original German translates literally as 'Nothing New in the West' and within the first 18 months of its publication it sold over 2.5 million copies in 22 languages, becoming one of the world's first international bestsellers. It is a short, sharp, infuriating novel about what it is like to be a soldier in hand-to-hand combat, told from a German point of view. The author's aim was 'to tell of a generation of men who, even though they may have escaped [its] shells, were destroyed by the war.' I will admit I didn't exactly like this book, but that's OK; instead, I hugely appreciated its literary and historical value and am glad to have experienced it, and that's plenty enough for me.

Top ten novels about the First World War *in case* All Quiet on the Western Front *leaves you wanting more*

1/William – an Englishman
by Cicely Hamilton (1919)
This is the greatest book ever written about the First World War and I will arm wrestle into submission anyone who argues otherwise. The scene where William and Griselda are on honeymoon and hear what they think is thunder, but is actually the guns of the German army, is genuinely unforgettable.

2/A Long Long Way
by Sebastian Barry (2005)
I love everything Barry writes and this is no exception. Willie Dunne leaves Dublin to go and fight for 'King, Country and Empire', leaving behind his intended, Gretta, and his policeman father.

3/Mrs Dalloway
by Virginia Woolf (1925)
Set in 1923, the novel considers the after-effects of the First World War on every aspect of British society, including the geranium beds.

4/Wake
by Anna Hope (2014)
Three women try to rebuild their personal lives while suffering from the devastating impact of the war. An easy, straightforward read, ideal for a long train journey accompanied by a weak cup of tea and a too-sweet biscuit.

5/The Good Soldier Svejk
by Jaroslav Hašek (1921)
This satirical Czech comedy about a professional dog thief serving in the Austro-Hungarian army during the First World War is odd but invigorating.

6/Under Fire
by Henri Barbusse (1917)
This novel about a group of French soldiers who volunteer to fight on the Western Front was the very first piece of narrative fiction to emerge from of the war. Fascinating, albeit very much a period piece.

7/A Farewell to Arms

by Ernest Hemingway (1929)
Hemingway invented a new way of utilizing language – detached, minimalist, staccato – to tell this wartime story of an American who drives ambulances for the Italian army and falls in love with an English nurse.

8/The Return of the Soldier

by Rebecca West (1918)
'Like most Englishwomen of my time, I was wishing for the return of a soldier': the first to address the subject, West's debut novel about the return of the shell-shocked Captain Baldry from the trenches of the First World War as told from the perspective of his cousin Jenny has an immediacy to it that is all but unsurpassed.

9/Birdsong

by Sebastian Faulks (1993)
This novel about a soldier fighting and loving and fighting and loving is a terrific read, despite being so sad. Particularly visceral are the hideous descriptions of the Battle of the Somme, among others.

10/Despised and Rejected

by Rose Allatini (1918)
A highly unusual story of a young gay man named Dennis who becomes a conscientious objector, refusing to fight in the war, as well as Antoinette as she gradually comes to the realization that she is a lesbian. Essentially a novel about tolerance.

Timeline: A brief whizz through some highlights in the development of magic realist novels *in case Morrison and Márquez leave you wanting more*

1925 German art critic Frank Roh first used the term '*magischer realismus*' to describe a new style of painting.

1935 *A Universal History of Infamy* by the Argentinian writer Jorge Luis Borges, who, with this collection of short stories in which magic happens within a realistic setting, is often perceived to have invented the genre in a literary context. This is controversial, however, because there are, of course, a number of other candidates – no movement emerges alone.

1967 *One Hundred Years of Solitude*, followed by *Chronicles of a Death Foretold* (1981) and *Love in the Time of Cholera* (1985), by Gabriel García Márquez. Márquez's many notable contributions mean he is often considered the 'father' of magic realism: he certainly gave it a distinctly Latin American spin.

1982 *The House of the Spirits* by Isabel Allende. Allende, who was born in Peru and grew up in Chile, where this novel is set, was one of the first to offer up magic realism from a female point of view in the course of telling this bewitching story of four generations of the Trueba family.

1984 *Nights at the Circus* by Angela Carter. Revel in the tale of a late-19th-century circus performer (an aerialist, to be precise) with actual real-life wings, blending realism with craziness in the most delightful of ways.

1990 *Like Water for Chocolate* by Laura Esquivel. Who knew that crying into a wedding cake could cause such havoc? This rather wonderful love story is full of clichés but entirely forgivable for it. Melodramatic, but that is sort of the point.

1994 *The Wind-Up Bird Chronicle* by Haruki Murakami. A guy's cat disappearing may not sound like much of a premise, but this bold, fantastical, Japanese novel pulls it off.

1996 *Primeval and Other Times* by Olga Tokarczuk. Set in a village in Poland that is guarded by four archangels. Hugely weird, hugely entertaining.

2019 *The Water Dancer* by Ta-Nehisi Coates. This ambitious novel, about a sensitive young man named Hiram who possesses magical powers, is full of big ideas at the same time as being a vivid evocation of the brutal reality of the slave system in mid-19th century Virginia.

January
February
March
April
May
June
July
August
September
October
November

December

It was snowing. It was always snowing at Christmas. December, in my memory, is white as Lapland, though there were no reindeers. But there were cats.

Dylan Thomas, *A Child's Christmas in Wales*
(1955)

I adore the month of December. Whatever your faith, culture or traditions, there is a sense of building towards a climax as you head towards the end of the calendar year. At the very least, this is a time of reflection. The misguided may start to wonder whether they are going to achieve all the goals they set themselves at the start of the year. The rest of us will just be thinking about how quickly another 12 months have passed during which we still failed to exercise as much as we had resolved to.

For some, December also brings the fun of the holiday season – a time of sequins, jolly jumpers and sparkly nail polish. We all have our favourite holiday traditions: mine arrives every year on 1 December when we carry the Christmas tree up the steep hill on the way to our house, my husband huffing and puffing and swearing while the rest of us giggle at him. This time of year can also have another dimension, though, of loneliness and isolation, which has been more intense than ever in recent times. So let us turn to novels to help get us through both the parties and the pauses, the discos and the dips – this is surely what novels are for.

Anna Karenina

BY LEO TOLSTOY (1878, RECOMMENDED
TRANSLATION 2000 BY RICHARD PEVEAR
AND LARISSA VOLOKHONSKY)

O K, bear with me: I am about to persuade you to pick up an 800-page Russian novel that frequently references 19th-century agricultural reform. But Tolstoy's *Anna Karenina* is, I promise you, a brilliantly gripping account of one woman's attempt to be true to herself. When you reach the end, you will feel more desperately alive in every cell in your body than you may have felt for a long time.

The plot of *Anna Karenina* mostly concerns the title character's love for Count Vronsky, a love that is doomed from the start due to the rigid moral strictures imposed on married women at the time by Russian society. No novel better captures the pain and torment of a love that cannot be:

> They've got no idea what happiness is, they don't know that without this love there is no happiness or unhappiness for us – there is no life.

Despite being known as one of the world's greatest love stories, *Anna Karenina* is clearly anti-romantic. Tolstoy mocked 'the marriage plot' that forms the basis of every romantic novel, once observing that the problem with the kinds of English family saga that he liked to read (Anthony Trollope, for example), was that they 'always end up with him putting his arm round her waist, then they get married, and he inherits an estate and a baronetcy...But a novel should not be about what happens before they get married, but what happens after they get married.' The unhappiness of Anna's marriage is balanced out by the happiness of other characters like Levin and Kitty, who more closely echo Tolstoy's own experience of matrimony. *Anna Karenina* is the most autobiographical of any of his writing, especially in matters of family life: his descriptions of breastfeeding, anxiously watching over a sick child or the sounds 'produced by what once was Kitty' as she struggles in labour are very much inspired by episodes in his own life.

I first read *Anna Karenina* aged 20 when I felt every thrilling emotion alongside Anna, cheerfully ignoring Tolstoy's theories about farming, with the exception of the description of Levin mowing grass all day with the peasants and finding happiness (or what we now call 'flow') while cutting 'another row, and yet another row, followed – long rows and short rows, with good grass and with poor grass...In the midst of his toil there were moments during which he forgot what he was doing, and it came all easy to him.' A few years later, cynical in the wake of an unhappy love affair, I saw Anna as the victim of a patriarchal society, seeking her freedom in Vronsky but denied escape. And on a third reading, as a parent, I appreciated the quiet domesticity of Levin and Kitty's story, as well as finally waking up to Levin's internal struggles. Tolstoy made 33 attempts at writing a novel about Peter the Great before starting *Anna Karenina*; it is only a slight exaggeration to say that in writing *Anna Karenina* he wrote 33 novels and each time you read it you will find something new and relevant to your own life.

I have one caveat: you must only – only – read the version that came out in 2000, translated by Richard Pevear and Larissa Volokhonsky. All others are as dullsville as can be. One is reminded, yet again, of the importance of translators, who are invariably underappreciated and yet obviously so crucial to whether we are able to enjoy world literature. Pevear and Volokhonsky's translation is by far the most readable one, and hence the most involving and moving.

Along with *Madame Bovary* by Gustave Flaubert (1856) and *Effi Briest* by Theodor Fontane (1895), which are basically the same book (thematically at least) about a woman led into misery by society's stupid rules, *Anna Karenina* is an appropriately melancholy, atmospheric, lengthy project to tackle in the month of December. Don't be daunted by how long/famous/Russian it is; I also give you full permission to skip the boring bits about agricultural reform or spiritual crises. What you will find when you do is a terribly sad tale about how painful it can be to fall in love, and more generally to be human, but set in a world of Russian parties and train stations and snowstorms that is so engrossing that it will stay with you for a long time afterwards. It also, most importantly, captures an essential human truth: 'All the variety, all the charm, all the beauty of life is made up of light and shadow.' Which, in many ways, is the very essence of December.

Diary of a Provincial Lady

BY E M DELAFIELD (1934)

Plant the indoor bulbs. Just as I am in the middle of them, Lady Boxe calls. I say, untruthfully, how nice to see her, and beg her to sit down while I just finish the bulbs...Lady B stays to tea. (Mem: Bread-and-butter too thick. Speak to Ethel.) We talk some more about bulbs, the Dutch School of Painting, Our Vicar's Wife, sciatica, and All Quiet on the Western Front. *(Query: Is it possible to cultivate the art of conversation when living in the country all the year round?).*

From the very first entry, *Diary of a Provincial Lady* declares its candidacy for the funniest book ever written. A fictional diary – whether that of Bridget Jones, Adrian Mole, a nobody, or a provincial lady – looks easy to write, but clearly is not. On the surface, the provincial lady's is full of domestic details and finds its comedy in the minutiae of the everyday, but look a little deeper and *au fond* it is an incisive and insightful commentary on the role of women in interwar society.

E M Delafield's background was conventionally aristocratic (moneyed, governesses, 'coming out'), but she rejected the 'good' marriage that was expected of her and retreated to a convent for a year (the setting for her early, dark, startling novel *Consequences* (1919)). When she emerged, she volunteered as a nurse throughout the First World War, after which she married a 'country gent' and had

two children. But the 'gent' was not a high earner and the two of them found that the money Delafield made from novels and journalism was vital to their comfortable-enough survival. So *Provincial Lady* is fairly autobiographical, but only fairly: for example, the real-life Robert cannot possibly have been as appalling as he appears in the book and was surely exaggerated in order to make readers think he was nothing to do with the original. But the details about children and food and clothes and hair and packing up the car and the relentless on-and-on-ness of many women's lives were true for E M Delafield and remain true for many of us (however much we try and pretend otherwise).

Behind the seemingly light tone of voice, there is a youngish woman deeply frustrated at the lot she has to endure as a result of her gender. Take, for example, her description of Christmas Day: 'Festive, but exhausting, Christmas. Robin and Vicky delighted with everything, and spend much of the day eating.' How sad that 'exhausting' is her primary response to what is supposed to be a day full of joy and fun, and yet many of us can empathize. Of course, the nameless heroine has a governess for the children and a cook and sordid questions of money are only mentioned in a humorous tone when there is not enough (once, for example, she has to pawn some jewellery), yet the book is infused with the thought: Why? Why is the dreadful Robert indulged and deferred to, while the provincial lady ties herself in knots trying to run the house, be nice to the children, be polite to the neighbours, in fact defer to everyone? Why would it be inconceivable for her to give it all up, to go AWOL for a few days, to do what she wants?

At the close of the first volume, the Provincial Lady reveals that:

Robert [husband] says, Why don't I get into Bed? I say, Because I am writing my Diary. Robert replies, kindly, but quite definitely,

*that in his opinion, That is Waste of Time. I get into bed and am
confronted by Query. Can Robert be right? Can only leave reply
to Posterity.*

Well, posterity has disagreed with Robert. *Diary of a Provincial
Lady* will quietly soothe the reader when she or he most needs
cheering up: it is the ideal book to get you through a stressful holiday
season. You are in for a treat.

CHRISTMAS PREPARATIONS

*He was coming at Christmas for five days. There had never
been such preparations. Paul and Arthur scoured the land
for holly and evergreens. Annie made the pretty paper
hoops in the old-fashioned way. And there was unheard-of
extravagance in the larder. Mrs Morel made a big and
magnificent cake. Then, feeling queenly, she showed Paul
how to blanch almonds. He skinned the long nuts
reverently, counting them all, to see not one was lost. It
was said that eggs whisked better in a cold place. So the
boy stood in the scullery, where the temperature was
nearly at freezing-point, and whisked and whisked, and
flew in excitement to his mother as the white of egg grew
stiffer and more snowy.*

D H Lawrence,
Sons and Lovers (1913)

Curl up by the fire with the finest historical fiction

The Secret River by Kate Grenville (2005)

This novel by a favourite Australian author of mine is historical fiction at its finest. Inspired by Grenville's own great-great-great-grandfather, it tells the story of William Thornhill, who in 1806 is convicted of stealing some timber from a barge on the River Thames and sentenced to be transported to Sydney, Australia, with his wife Sarah and two young children. Grenville's narrative is marvellously engaging, entertaining and thought-provoking, as well as fascinating about what life in Sydney was like in the earliest days of white settlement. And, like the best historical fiction, it will then make you want to read all the non-fiction you can lay your hands on about the early history of Australia, too.

A murder mystery as grim as the weather outside

The Midnight Witness by Sara Blaedel (2018)

In the first in a series of best-selling novels originally written in Danish and featuring homicide detective Louise Rick, a journalist is found dead in the backyard of the Royal Hotel in Copenhagen on the same day that a young woman is found dead in the park. What's the connection? Set in winter in Copenhagen as rain falls under the glow of streetlamps in dark alleyways, it features everything else you would expect from a classic detective novel but with a distinctly 21st-century spin to it.

Top five ice-cold novels

1/*The Evenings*
by Gerard Reve (1947)
This one-of-a-kind Dutch comic novel about life in the suburbs of Amsterdam is set in December 1946. Twenty-something Frits lives with his parents and his job recalls Jack Lemmon's in the film *The Apartment*: 'I take cards out of a file,' then, 'once I have taken them out, I put them back in again.' He spends his evenings wandering the streets in search of meaning and it is in all honesty kind of boring, but in a very soothing and intentional way and thus a rather lovely break from much of contemporary fiction.

2/*Moon of the Crusted Snow*
by Waubgeshig Rice (2018)
A chilly, chilling novel about a small indigenous community in northern Canada that gets cut off during a particularly challenging winter, then slowly realizes they've missed the Apocalypse...

3/*Christmas Pudding*
by Nancy Mitford (1932)
A silly, posh, period piece, but like a farce it consistently delivers on its jokes as Mitford's larger-than-life characters spend Christmas swanning around the Cotswolds in the snow being mildly ridiculous.

4/*Snow*
by John Banville (2020)
Imagine a poet writes a murder mystery – this is that book. Banville gorgeously evokes a sense of chilliness, not just in terms of temperature but also in terms of the atmosphere of post-Second World War rural Ireland.

5/*The Ice Palace*
by Tarjei Vesaas (1963)
Two 11-year-old girls are fascinated by a frozen waterfall in the Norwegian fjords. Uncompromising, icy and a little like a fairytale in its simplicity.

Jane Austen
A cliché for a reason

Who better to read in December than Jane Austen? Not just because it is her birthday month, but because her books are an unbeatable mix of romance and parties and dresses and witticisms – almost everything you could possibly want for the festive season. She incorporates Christmas into every single one of her six full-length novels too, for example in this family scene from *Persuasion* (1817):

> *On one side was a table occupied by some chattering girls, cutting up silk and gold paper; and on the other were tressels and trays, bending under the weight of brawn and cold pies, where riotous boys were holding high revel; the whole completed by a roaring Christmas fire, which seemed determined to be heard, in spite of all the noise of the others.*

She writes enticingly about all kinds of celebrations, in fact. In the Regency world she depicts, balls often last for hours and hours: in *Sense and Sensibility* (1811), Marianne hears that Willoughby danced 'from eight o'clock till four, without once sitting down'. Such fun! It is a fool's project to attempt to rank Austen's novels because each has its own strengths and, honestly, they are all brilliant, even *Northanger Abbey* (1817) once you remember it is intended to be a satire and hence over the top. Personally, I adore *Sense and Sensibility*; meanwhile, *Pride and Prejudice* (1813) is a cliché for a reason and if you haven't re-read it within the last decade, I implore you to do so immediately.

Focus on...

.

Postscript

I hope that, in the course of reading *The Literary Almanac*, you have found many, many novels to add to your TBR (To Be Read) list. Whether you plan to read them laid out on a beach towel on holiday or snuggled up by the fire on a Sunday afternoon, there will no doubt be some you'll love, some you'll hate, and some you'll irrationally dismiss for no reason (don't worry, we've all done it) – but surely that's half the fun? Either way, I am confident you will feel inspired anew.

A novel read at the perfect moment has the potential to be truly transformative. So much of our life is defined by the seasons; why not our literary life, too? Novels teach us how to understand the world. Without them, we are lost. They are what define us from other animals. I mean, have you ever seen a chimpanzee clutching a copy of David Foster Wallace's *Infinite Jest* to his chest just to try to impress a mate? No, you have not.

And so here we are. One of my favourite last lines in literature is from *Middlemarch* by George Eliot (1871): 'The growing good of the world is partly dependent on unhistoric acts; and that things are not so ill with you and me as they might have been is half owing to the number who lived faithfully a hidden life, and rest in unvisited tombs.'

The following from *The Makioka Sisters* by Jun'ichiro Tanizaki (1948) is also pretty spectacular in its own way: 'Yukiko's diarrhea persisted through the twenty-sixth, and was a problem on the train to Tokyo.' My least favourite? Well, in all honesty I am no huge fan of 'So we beat on, boats against the current, borne back ceaselessly into the past', which is from *The Great Gatsby* by F Scott Fitzgerald (1925), of course.

But that's the thing with last lines – in fact, with endings in general. They're tricky...

Right?

 ...

Index

191

Credits

Page 11, reproduced with permission of The Society of Authors as the Literary Representative of the Estate of Virginia Woolf

Page 40, extract from *The Single Hound: Poems of a Lifetime* ed. Martha Dickinson Bianchi (1914)

Page 53, extract from 'The Waste Land' by T.S. Eliot (1922) reproduced with permission of Faber and Faber Ltd.

Page 111, extract from *The Journals of Sylvia Plath* (2014) reproduced with permission of Faber and Faber Ltd.

Page 173, extract from *A Child's Christmas in Wales* (1955) by Dylan Thomas, reproduced with permission of David Higham Associates. ©The Dylan Thomas Trust.